GREAT IRISH LOVE STORIES

BY

UNA MORRISSY

THE MERCIER PRESS
DUBLIN and CORK

The Mercier Press Limited
4 Bridge Street, Cork
25 Lower Abbey Street, Dublin 1

© The Mercier Press

First Printed 1959
This edition 1976

ISBN 85342 473 X

Reproduced photo-litho and printed in the Republic
of Ireland by Cahill (1976) Limited, East Wall Road,
Dublin 3.

CONTENTS

Parnell and Kitty O'Shea

WHEN A MAN relinquishes all for the love of a lady, the world takes him warmly to its heart. He has the noble proportions of tragedy. Even if the love, or the lady, are a little less than noble, he is not diminished, as the romantic interest in unfortunate lovers from Mark Antony to the Duke of Windsor proves. But if he has everything filched from him through the chicanery and chicken-heartedness of others, because he loves, he is only grotesque. He is no longer a giant, but a fool. Parnell was considered both in his lifetime, and long after, by vociferous and vituperative partisans. Perhaps the shouting will never altogether die down, perhaps he might start an argument to-day. But with the blinding mists of passion and prejudice dissolved in time, it is easier now to regard the 'affaire' with Kitty O'Shea from his viewpoint, purely and simply as a love affair.

Of course, as Wilde has wittily observed, 'the truth is rarely pure and never simple.' It was only the strength of Parnell's passion and the totality of his nature which led him to look upon, as a simple private matter, one of the most tortuous and potentially explosive relationships it would be possible to encounter.

On a warm sunny afternoon in July of 1880, the House of Commons was debating the Compensation for Disturbance Bill, a humane piece of legislation introduced by the Liberal Chief Secretary for Ireland, for the relief of evicted tenants. It was rather too humane for the House, which was busy adding nullifying amendments, and the Nationalist Party were present in force to save what they could of it. As Parnell listened to the debate he was handed a card informing him that two ladies who wished to see him were waiting in the Palace Yard.

One of the names was familiar. Parnell was used to attempts

to lionise him, and extremely deft at foiling them, and he had been dodging the political dinners given by the charming Mrs. O'Shea for months. Her husband, Captain Willie, had successfully posed as a Home Ruler in the recent election, and been returned, under the wing of the O'Gorman Mahon for County Clare. Now Katie was in politics for Willie's sake, as she had been in Spanish mines a little earlier, and she was determined to have the 'Uncrowned King of Ireland' grace her board.

If he were not already stubbornly inaccessible, Parnell would certainly have absented himself from the O'Shea's, for his opinion of Willie had been formed when he encountered him during the election. He took in his dandified appearance, his unconcealed indifference to Irish matters, his obvious insincerity and observed: 'That's just the kind of man we *don't* want in the Party!' But he reckoned without Katie O'Shea. He had reckoned without her persistence in the matter of luring him to her house, and when he stepped out into the Palace Yard in the sunshine, to render his refusals more firmly absolute, he reckoned without her good looks and her charm.

He saw not an overbearing social greyhound pouncing on her prey, but a pretty, gracious, softly-curved young woman, who combined diffidence with dignity, and concealed an indefatigable determination under a reassuring sympathy. She was all woman, and Parnell was instantly captivated.

He was not a callow youth and he had met plenty of beautiful women before—far more beautiful than Katie. He was quite normally susceptible, though not usually to other men's wives, and he was more than capable of ruthlessly suppressing anything which might prove a social or political impediment. Yet he was and remained for the rest of his life helplessly enthralled by Katie.

The icy aloofness which was characteristic of Parnell, concealed a sensitive, introspective temperament, very easily hurt and a prey to prolonged spells of black depression. Constitutionally he was frail and his propensity to overwork himself had run his health down to a low level in 1880, which had seen the conclusion of an exhausting trip to the States to raise funds, and the successful electioneering campaign which returned him in triumph for Cork, Meath and Mayo. His only other serious love affair had resulted in a humiliating fiasco. Since that time he had more or less lost interest in women except for occasional desultory encounters which satisfied a temporary sexual urge, but gave him no affection and left him more bleakly alone than before. Such taut, vulnerable natures need affection and sympathy in even greater quantities than the average human being. Despite a large and volatile family, Charles Stewart Parnell was a very lonely man. And so it was into the vacuum that nature abhors that Katie entered with such consoling warmth on that sunny summer afternoon.

There was nothing moody or introspective about Katie. Notwithstanding her generous curves, her sensuous mouth and large sympathetic eyes, she was a woman of ceaseless mental and physical activity. She had a good brain, a devouring ambition and a rich capacity for intrigue. She was the motive power behind the O'Shea partnership, and she had to be, for Willie's gifts were of a purely speculative character. One wonders where, if she had married a man of talent and ability, she might have stopped.

Her marriage to Willie was a queer, chequered, passionate, quarrelsome affair. Though he had married her for love, they had nothing at all in common. Katie was by way of being an intellectual, while Willie's interests lay in racing, gambling and dubious business enterprises. He alternated between poverty and affluence, though his spending powers never diminished, and Katie did not appreciate the insecurity which went with Willie's charm. Yet the charm was there, and Katie was subject to it always. He was a cosmopolite and Katie was no bohemian. His idea of married life was to maintain bachelor apartments in Town or on the Continent, while his wife and children lived in the country. They quarrelled a great deal, but Katie had a rich old aunt who merited Willie's attention, and Willie had a constant physical attraction for Katie, so they maintained a relationship of wary intimacy, which continued unbroken, even by Parnell, for many years.

In fairness to Katie, it must be stated that her idea in pursuing Parnell with invitations to partake of her extremely good cuisine, was wholly to advance Willie's political career. When Willie became interested in an enterprise Katie endeared herself to the influential people connected with it. While this amiable arrangement usually resulted in a little entertainment for the neglected Katie, and the expenditure of plenty of money on Willie's project, it had so far failed to put Willie on a really firm basis. But Katie believed in Willie, and was sure that he lacked only a suitable opening for his talents. She was delighted when he thought of politics. Naturally neither of them knew or cared anything about Home Rule. Indeed, Willie, though born in Dublin, despised his origins. But it was easier and cheaper to run for an Irish than an English constituency. Katie coaxed the money out of Mrs. Benjamin Wood, her rich benefactress, and Willie's political career, with its fateful results for Ireland, was launched.

Whether or not she felt the same electric spark which quivered through Parnell on that memorable July day outside the House of Commons it is hard to say, but over thirty years later, when the glamour was gone, and even the mud-slinging forgotten, she was able to write 'of how he came out into the Palace Yard, a tall, gaunt figure, thin and deadly pale, and how he looked straight at me smiling, with his curiously burning eyes looking into mine with an intentness that threw into my brain the sudden thought: "This man is wonderful and different".'

The bond of sympathy, at any rate, was immediate. Katie had an immense capacity for mothering people, and the lonesome-looking handsome man went straight to her heart. She teased him a little about avoiding her invitations and was rewarded by hearing him ask to be allowed to dine with her on his return from Paris, where he was going immediately. As they said goodbye, she dropped a rose she had been wearing and saw him pick it up, put it to his lips and into his buttonhole. When he was dead the rose was found among his most private papers. They began to meet regularly, at his suite in the Westminster Palace Hotel, or at her sister's house; they might take a box at the Opera, or if the evening were fine and the debate not important, they would hire a hansom and drive down in the summer cool to Richmond. Willie was delighted. Parnell, who in the normal course would scarcely have noticed his existence, was now obliged to be courteous to him, and Willie even hoped for advancement in the Party. Chief Secretary for Ireland became the goal of his ambitions, though he did not trouble to hide his opposition to the Land League. Parnell now started on the long, tortuous journey of intrigue, blackmail, deception and lies which terminated in his ruin, and brought to ashes the flame of Irish hopes for freedom.

To do him justice, none of the backstairs business of the next ten years was his doing. He saw no point in complicating a situation which seemed plain enough to him. But again he was reckoning without Mrs. O'Shea. It was characteristic of Parnell that when he took a step he took it for all time and could never be deflected from his course. His love for Katie was so complete, and within its framework so honest, that he assumed the same unconditional response on her part. In that, to say the least of it, he was naive. No matter how great her emotional affinity with him, Mrs. O'Shea was not free to jettison her family responsibilities. There would certainly have had to be some delays and difficulties for she had several children, and Willie was no provider. Yet the difficulties were not insuperable. Parnell wanted her to divorce Willie and marry him, a logical enough step, since they were both Protestants. True it would probably have lost him the leadership of Irish affairs, but it would never have brought the resounding crash of the alternative course. But Katie was not of the stuff of heroes. Unfortunately for himself and for the country he served, Parnell sold himself body and soul to a woman with the financial outlook of a minor bourgeois black marketeer. She was incapable of understanding why she could not have her cake and eat it too. And so for ten years she contrived by every possible manoeuvre to do both.

Divorce was out of the question, she said, while Mrs. Benjamin Wood was alive. She had set Katie up in a house near her own, on condition that Katie was to be her companion. The scandal of divorce would mean that she would immediately disinherit her, and all the careful work she and Willie had been putting in for years would be lost, and their children would have no future security. Parnell accepted the argument. Infatuated as he was he had no alternative. But he found Willie a more difficult pill to swallow. From the time, around October of 1880, that they became lovers, he regarded Katie as his wife, and Willie as the cuckoo in the nest. He had some justification for this attitude. Willie could scarcely be called a homelover. As Parnell made known ten years later, it could be 'proved that in the twenty-three years of Mr. O'Shea's married life he spent only four hundred days in his own home,' and presumably even fewer nights. But Katie talked him into Willie too. Willie could be useful, she said, and otherwise he might turn nasty and provoke a public scandal which would have the same effect on Aunt Ben as a divorce.

At first there was no question of Willie turning nasty. He was more than content. His attitude to Katie's relations with gentlemen of influence was quite cynical, and he had a healthy respect for the prejudices of Aunt Ben. He encouraged Katie in every way to entertain Parnell. He wanted preferment and Parnell was just the man he needed to know. 'Take him back with you to Eltham,' he would tell Katie. 'Make him all happy and comfortable for the night, and just get him to agree.' And Katie was born to make people comfortable.

Not the least of her fascination for Parnell was the genuinely affectionate care with which she looked after his health, his appetite, his general well-being. He soon got into the habit of driving down to Eltham after a late sitting at the House, and he would arrive to find a cosy lamp-lit room, his jacket and slippers warming by the fire, and a delicious little meal, prepared by Katie, who was a superb cook. He could relax immediately in the warmth and comfort, and Katie made sure never to bother him with small talk or worries, but encouraged him to eat in silent contentment. He was quite unused to these little feminine attentions. He had lived most of his life indifferent to food and comfort, and Katie added a new dimension to his life. A man who badly needed mothering had chosen a woman in whom the maternal instinct was developed beyond all her other qualities. To such a man the thought of being thrown again on his own inadequate resources, in a world which admired his astonishing outward composure and knew nothing of his

inner insecurity and conflicts, was intolerable. He was prepared
to accept any bargain as long as it left him Katie.

He soon found that there was more to Willie than tolerating
him in the Party and accepting him as part, however casual,
of Katie's domestic scene. Among Willie's less endearing
qualities, and they were many, were his propensities for being
a dog in the manger and a blackmailer. Having encouraged
Katie all he could to attract Parnell, he was angered to discover
that she was actually enjoying herself. Though he had system-
atically neglected her, and the home to which he contributed
nothing for years, his vanity was stung by the discovery that the
distant, haughty Irishman was her frequent guest. Using a
suitcase belonging to Parnell as an excuse, he made a righteous
scene which provoked Katie to a furious anger in which she
announced that she loved Parnell. It was a foolish gesture for
the cautious Katie, and it cost her dear. Willie, still clad in
his ill-fitting mantle of outraged virtue, challenged Parnell
to a duel, which to his astonishment and dismay Parnell accepted.
He had quite a job to wriggle out of it, but he managed to frighten
Katie with thoughts of injury to Parnell and played the old trump
card of the scandal to Aunt Ben. So Katie did some more
wheedling and manoeuvring, and the situation was resolved
in a way much more pleasing to Willie—by a cheque. Many
years later, William O'Brien said that if Parnell had merely
produced the stubs of his cheque books half of the charges of
the Divorce Case would have fallen through.

Parnell would have nothing to do with these negotiations.
He was so dominated by Katie that he agreed to any conditions
she herself proposed, but he refused then or at any other time
to descend to bargaining over her with Willie. Willie, of course,
resented this aloofness bitterly, and his shallow, spiteful nature
became filled with a personal loathing for the Irish leader which
would never really be satisfied but by revenge.

Having clarified the situation in his own mind at least, Parnell
spent all his leisure with Katie. She was to be seen regularly
in the Strangers' Gallery listening to the debates, and he would
always, by a gesture with his handkerchief, or the flower in his
buttonhole, indicate his immediate awareness of her presence.

Sometimes, for a week or so they would escape from the claims of Aunt Ben and the children to Brighton, which he liked. If he were tied to the House she would come up to his hotel suite and prepare a dainty meal in his private sitting room. If he were journeying to Ireland she would be there in the draughty old station waiting room to be with him to the last minute. He could not bear to be deprived of her company and if for any reason they were separated, he sent her a goodnight telegram every night. During the Spring of 1882, their first child, a little girl who survived only a few weeks, was born. Parnell was in Kilmainham Gaol at the time, greatly agitated by fears for Katie's health, excitement over his approaching parenthood and intense gloom over Willie's presence in London, which was obnoxious to him and, he feared, a strain on Katie. It says volumes for Katie's command of a situation which would have daunted most women, that during all this time Willie remained convinced that the child was his.

Between keeping the rich autocratic Aunt Ben, the petulant insatiable Willie and the morbid and highly-strung Parnell contented Katie should have surely have turned into a crank herself. But her values being material rather than spiritual, she was better able to shrug off the personal conflicts which normally shatter more sensitive natures. She lost none of her charms or her enthusiasms, and she continued with unfailing optimism to hope that the entire organisation of the Irish Nationalist Party could be tailored to fit Willie—and thus bring security to them all.

Katie's price was very high. Parnell was the only man of his turbulent period who was able to stand back from and above the embittering circumstances of the Land War, the Coercion Acts and all the paraphernalia of deliberate misgovernment. His ambitions were for nothing less than the complete freedom of Ireland to govern herself, but he knew how to wait. He was able by the magnetism of his personality to control the very diverse elements in the Party which ranged from extreme Fenianism on the one hand, to diehard constitutionalism on the other. It was a herculean task, but he managed it, and there is no doubt that the sympathy and love of Katie brought

him happiness and relief. It was nothing less than tragic that
his already grave burdens should be ludicrously weighted with
the get-rich-quick ambitions of a cheap political opportunist. Had
he been of a more extrovert temperament, the terrible intensity
of his passion would have evaporated somewhat in the healthier
atmosphere of congenial associations and friendships. But
he shunned society, made few friendships and no confidants
at all. Katie alone received his confidences, and with sublime
faith in herself and Willie, and a shattering ignorance of the
Irish situation, intrigued and schemed, nagged and pleaded
with everyone from Gladstone down, who could find a political
plum for Willie, and, incidentally, advance Parnell's ambitions
for Home Rule.

In 1884 she invited both Parnell and Willie to spend a holiday
with her in Brighton, where they could discuss a proposal for
a Local Government Bill, the pet scheme of Joseph Chamberlain.
It cannot, one feels, have been a relaxing spell at the seaside
for any of them. The cold disdain of Parnell mixed with the
peevish truculence of Willie must have called all Katie's dip-
lomatic talents into play. Willie was Chamberlain's go-between.
But vast though his talents were for the art of the double-cross,
he was a bad intermediary. His lack of moral fibre made him
alter that which he had not the courage to transmit, and the
people who used him were apt to find that their proposals had
been garbled or even omitted entirely if Willie deemed it prudent.
The duality of Parnell's role in Brighton can hardly be imagined.
Forced by Katie's financial aspirations to tolerate Willie's officious
and ineffectual interference in the political arena, he coolly
ignored his position as Katie's lawful husband. No doubt he
felt entitled to value for his cheques. A year after his death,
Katie records, not without a certain relish, a domestic scene
that occurred. 'One evening when Captain O'Shea and Mr.
Parnell had been discussing some important matter, the three
of us dined together. As the night drew on I retired before
the others, and my door was still left standing open when Captain
O'Shea, who was the second to retire, came upstairs. He spoke
to me, and the discussion of the evening's debate began afresh,
and in the course of it he entered my room and the door closed

Suddenly the door was banged violently open and Mr. Parnell stalked in, his head held high and his eyes snapping; he said not a word, but marched straight up to me, picked me up, threw me over his shoulder and turned on his heel; still without a word he marched out of the room across the landing and into his own room, where he threw me down on the bed and shut the door.'

So the long haggle went on. We have the spectacle of Parnell absenting himself during a vital election campaign from Ireland, in order to force Willie down the throats of the electors in Liverpool. He was defeated by a majority of 55 votes which nearly killed him. Katie was distracted. She wept and nagged and entreated. Willie would ruin them all if he were not placated. And indeed he intended to. 'I have been treated in blackguard fashion,' he wrote to Katie, 'and I mean to hit back a stunner. I have everything ready; no drugs could make me sleep last night, and I packed my shell with dynamite. It cannot hurt my friend (Chamberlain) and it will send a blackguard's reputation with his deluded country into smithereens.' The Party were aghast when Parnell announced his intention of running Willie for Galway. It very nearly cost him the leadership of the Party and the support of the adoring nation. Joseph Biggar and Tim Healy went before him to Galway, and Biggar went so far as to tell the electors that Parnell was giving the seat to O'Shea because he was the husband of Parnell's mistress. But the magnetism of Parnell and the fear of losing all hope of Home Rule held their loyalties. In a dramatic gesture Parnell stretched out his hand towards his Galway listeners: 'I have Home Rule for Ireland in the hollow of my hand. If you dispute my decision now the English will say "Parnell's power is broken" and that will be the end of the Home Rule movement.' So Willie scraped in and was kept quiet for another while, until his political career perished between the Scylla of voting for Gladstone's Home Rule Bill and the Charybdis of losing Chamberlain's support if he did. His abstention threw him out of the Party for ever.

It seems at times as if the story of Parnell's love for Katie becomes the story of finding a niche for Willie. At no time was their life untrammelled by some unpleasant factor, and it says a good deal for the quality of his devotion that it survived the terrible demands made upon it. Where Katie was concerned, of course, he was an incurable romantic, and his chivalry was aroused by the thought of what she was forced to endure in being married, even if in name only, to Willie. That she did not find Willie as totally objectionable as he did was one of the things she managed very skilfully to hide.

In 1886 came the sensational Pigott forgeries and Parnell Commission which vindicated the Irish leader, and abashed, though only temporarily, the pontifical and infallible *Times*. Parnell suspected Willie's hand somewhere in the plot, and sure enough he came to light in his old capacity as go-between. It was obvious that if Aunt Ben's and Parnell's money were strong enough barriers to open scandal, Willie was going to lose no opportunity of revenge. A curious sidelight on Willie's connection with Pigott which has never been explained was that the last person to see Pigott alive in Madrid, a few hours before he shot himself, was Willie.

The complete vindication of the Commission was one of Parnell's greatest personal triumphs. When he first entered the House after the dramatic downfall of Pigott, every Nationalist and Liberal and even some Tory members rose to cheer him. On occasions such as this Parnell's supreme qualities of leadership shone with a brilliance that justified the idolatrous loyalty he could inspire. Sir Edward Clarke described the scene later: 'I saw Mr. Parnell standing erect among the whole standing crowd. He took no notice of it whatever. When they had finished standing up they sat down, and he took no notice of their rising up or of their sitting down. And when they had resumed their places he proceeded to make a perfectly calm and quiet speech in which he made not the smallest reference direct or indirect to the incident. I thought as I looked at him that night that that man was a born leader of men—calm, self-confident and powerful.' Only his friends knew of the nervous convulsion of his hands behind his back, and only Katie knew of his moments of despair such as came over him during one of their trips to Brighton. He caught her up in his arms one day and swung her over the edge of the pier above the swirling waters, with that queer red light that glowed in his eyes at times when he was deeply moved. 'Oh, my wife, my wife,' he said to her, 'I believe I'll jump in with you, and we shall be free for ever.'

Katie rejoiced in his triumph. She was unable to be present at the sittings in the House because Mrs. Benjamin Wood was dying, but Parnell told her all about it. He shrewdly interpreted much of the personal acclaim to a certain English smugness at the fairness of the Commission which had ended by honouring the man it set out to defile. 'They only howl with joy,' he told her, 'because I have been found within the law.' 'But,' persisted Katie, 'don't you feel a little excited and proud when they all cheer you, really you?' 'Yes,' he answered, 'when it is really me, when I am in the midst of a peasant crowd in Ireland, then I feel a little as I do when I see you smile across the street at me before we meet. Don't be too pleased with the clappings of these law lovers, Queenie. I have a presentiment that you will hear them another way before long.'

The Home Rule cause reached the peak of its possibilities with the success of the Parnell Commission. Parnell was made a freeman of Edinburgh and was almost as well-known in London as in Dublin. He remained very sceptical of the genuineness of the goodwill, and the subsequent reaction when the Divorce case came up, proved him right. Aunt Ben finally died at the age of about 99. After matters immediately relating to her death were cleared up, Parnell and Katie made their home in Brighton, which agreed with his health. It appeared as if Katie had reaped the reward of her devotion, for the old lady left her the entire fortune amounting to about a quarter of a million. But the triumph was illusory and brief.

Willie was out for blood. His hatred for Parnell increased proportionately with the Irish leader's success, and the disposition of Aunt Ben's will meant that after all his care and ten years' wait, he had no real claim on a penny. But Katie knew her Willie, and she knew that a substantial sum would buy out even his passion for revenge. Most unfortunately there had to be a delay. The various Wood relations disputed the will which meant that the probate period had to be extended. Katie elicited that £20,000 would have compensated Willie for all his troubles, and if she could have got her hands on it from any source, the history of Home Rule might have been different. But she could not, and Willie sued for the divorce that Parnell had wanted ten years earlier.

The shrewdest and grimmest protagonist in political life, Parnell, like most romantics, was easy-going to the point of naiveté in his private affairs. Had he brought the same vision to bear on his personal as on his public problems, O'Shea's appearance in the Divorce Court could have been as ignominious as Pigott's before the Commission. But he wanted only to marry Katie and secure the custody of their two children. As Katie put it: 'Mr. Parnell insisted that there must be a divorce so that he could marry me. It was a matter that touched his pride. Apart altogether from our love, he could not bear that my name should be compromised through him. He would do nothing—assist in nothing—consent to nothing that would prevent the divorce talking place, and he would have nothing to do with any discussions as to a settlement, with any negotiations as to a way out except on the basis of there being a divorce. Yet with all this he left me to act as I thought best for myself and my children.'

So once more Katie's bourgeois instincts were in command and she made every blunder in the book, from quarrelling with her lawyer to charging Willie with adultery with her own sister, an action which to put it cynically was not only a crime but a mistake, for it alienated all public sympathy. To do her justice, however, she was no part of Parnell's refusal to fight. She begged him to, but he was adamant. 'What's the use?' he would say. 'We want a divorce, and divorce or not, I shall always come where you are.'

On November 15, 1890, the case of O'Shea v. O'Shea came before the Divorce Court. If Katie had not so wildly brought the counter-accusations, the case need never have taken the sordid turn which shocked public opinion. She gave a heaven-sent opening to the opposing counsel to probe deeply into her relations with Parnell and drag them out, in false perspective, to the public eye. Parnell's various ruses and disguises, of which he was always fond, for avoiding political publicity became the guilty aliases and furtive shufflings of the home-breaker and the cad. The pungent irony of anyone out-smarting Willie in the arts of seduction cannot have been lost on any of their contemporaries. But so entrenched was the hatred of Parnell and Irish Nationalism that even Willie's conjugal rights were good enough to uphold if they were powerful enough to pull down Parnell. Winston Churchill has crystallised the English sentiment with unabashed candour in his biography of his father, Lord Randolph Churchill: 'Her Majesty's Government regained in the Divorce Court the credit they had lost before the Special Commission.'

But the combined artillery of all the hostile elements could not have broken the Irish cause were it not for the defection of Parnell's own colleagues, a departure he had never anticipated no matter how bad the outlook. The tragic history of the Parnell split is not for discussion here, except for its adverse effect on his health which dramatically shortened his life. Confident in his own greatly superior ability to lead the Irish cause, Parnell determined to fight every inch of the way. Week after week he journeyed from Brighton to different parts of Ireland to address the people, to urge their unity, to force them to look at the question in its entirety, always hurrying back to spend the week-end with Katie. The strain told terribly on his indifferent health, and he would return to Katie exhausted in body and mind.

On June 25, 1891, they were married in a little Sussex registry office. With his usual determination to avoid the press, he told a manservant he would require him at the registry office at eleven to act as a witness. He sent him to have his breakfast in readiness, while he and Mrs. O'Shea drove to the registry office an hour earlier. On their way back they pulled up the hood of the phaeton and had the pleasure of seeing the pressmen, who had, of course, extracted the information from the servant, pass them at full speed for the eleven o'clock appointment. There were some gathered outside the house and to them he said simply: 'Let Mrs. Parnell pass. I'll see you presently.'

That evening he said to Katie: 'The storms and the thunderings will never hurt us now, Queenie, my wife, for there is nothing in the wide world that can be greater than our love; there is nothing in all the world but you and I.'

His marriage cost him the Irish clergy. They found the re-marriage of Mrs. O'Shea very objectionable, and the remnant of their thinning ranks turned against him. But Parnell did not expect an easy victory and as in previous campaigns he knew how to fight with an eye on the last battle.

But alas for his long-term policy and for Katie's ten-year plan for keeping and eating her cake. Although he was barely forty-five, his delicate constitution worn down by years of hard work, irregular hours, intense nervous strain and travel in all weathers, gave way. In September of 1891, crippled with rheumatism and hardly able to speak with pain, he addressed a crowd in Roscommon in a steady downpour. 'If I had taken the advice of my doctor,' he told the cheering crowd, 'I should have gone to bed when I arrived in Dublin, but if I had done that my enemies would be throwing up their hats and announcing that I was dead before I was buried.' Returning to Dublin, he addressed a crowd before leaving for the mail, promising to come back 'next Saturday week.' Then too ill to travel, but determined to get back to Katie he left for Brighton. When he arrived he was so weak that she had to help him into the house where he almost collapsed. 'O my wife,' he said, 'it is good to be back. You may keep me a bit now.'

For a week Katie nursed him with all her skill. They made plans for their new house, and for continuing his fight to reunite Irish opinion. But his heart was unable to stand up to the strain of the fever. In the evening of October 6, 1891, after a day of lying with his eyes closed, 'just smiling if I touched him,' says Katie, he opened his eyes and said: 'Kiss me, sweet Wifie, and I will try to sleep a little.'

'I lay down by his side, and kissed the burning lips he pressed to mine for the last time. The fire of them fierce beyond any I had ever felt, even in his most loving moods, startled me, and as I slipped my hand from under his head, he gave a little sigh, and became unconscious. The doctor came at once, but no remedies prevailed against this sudden failure of the heart's action, and my husband died without regaining consciousness, before his last kiss was cold on my lips.'

He returned to Ireland, as he had promised, but in his coffin. In the tempestuous grief of the people who mourned him, there was the unity for which he had worked so hard.

Poor Katie had another thirty years to live. For all her depressing devotion to money, she had really loved him and in a way when he died she died too. After her careful attention to Aunt Ben, the will was successfully contested, chiefly as the result of the divorce case, and thirty-five relatives were satisfied before she got her share. Even then she got a substantial sum, but she had Willie's extravagance, and there was at least one bankruptcy charge against her. She became interested in spiritualism and carried on long 'conversations' with Parnell.

Her greatest crime was the publication of his letters twenty-three years after his death. They were not literary masterpieces, but foolish, intimate confessions intended for her eyes alone. In this violation of their private relationship, one sees again the mediocre stature of the woman fate selected for a giant role.

James Clarence Mangan and
Margaret Stackpoole

Go on, to tell how, with genius wasted,
Betrayed in friendship, befooled in love,
With spirit shipwrecked, and young hopes blasted,
       He still, still strove.

So wrote James Clarence Mangan of himself, in the haunted
poem, *The Nameless One*, and opened a controversy which
none, even of his contemporaries, has been able finally to close.
Two women attracted him in a lifetime spent in back streets,
garrets and public houses, and it is possible that had the one
lived or the other loved him, his spectre-haunted, wretched
existence might have been charged with colour and hope and
life.

While in his twenties and earning a pittance in a solicitor's
office, he endeavoured to supplement his income by contributions
to various journals and magazines, and by tuition in foreign
languages. He was appointed German tutor to a young girl
called Catherine Hayes, who lived with her parents at a place
called Rehoboth House on the south side of Dublin. She seems
to have been a young lady of considerable charm and warmth
of character, and Mangan, the shy recluse, opened and flowered
in her company and under the radiance of her interest and
sympathy for his hopes and dreams. Though she was very
considerably younger than himself, and there was no question
of his being in love with her, the friendship had a tender quality
which enriched his days, and lightened a little the terrible
depressions to which he was a constant prey. Incurably introspective, shrinking from the inevitable blows and buffets of
life which Mangan always felt were especially intensified for

him, he felt a confidence and a sense of comfort in Catherine's youthful and affectionate presence. Unfortunately for her poet-tutor, the poor girl died at a very early age, and her untimely death deepened and strengthened his melancholia. He felt her loss acutely, and was convinced that fate had yet again singled him out for a crushing blow. 'His sorrow was intense,' says a contemporary and friend, James Price. 'He literally would not be comforted. The gloom of his spirit seemed from this period to become more settled.'

Around this same time, when he was about thirty, Mangan became acquainted with a family living in Ranelagh, of which there were three daughters. Their name was Stackpoole, and with Margaret, who was about ten years younger than himself, Mangan fell wholly and passionately in love. Though there are two or three versions of the ending of his only love affair, everyone seems agreed that at the beginning it went well, and that Mangan was favourably received by the young lady.

It is only when we consider the almost unbearable intensity of Mangan's emotions, his diffidence, and his conviction that doom, frustration and defeat lay in wait for him at all times, that we may appreciate how glorious, and how dangerous it is for such a man to yield himself up to the fiery crucible of human love. Creative artist and poet, he might have emerged from the experience, however it ended, strengthened and enriched; but for Mangan the adventure was fraught with dire possibilities.

For a little while he walked with the angels. A semi-biographical article which he published in a Dublin magazine later, gives his own account of that rapturous interlude. 'I avowed my passion,' he says, 'and was not rejected. Changed as I am in heart and soul, I look back upon the dazzling brightness of that brief hour with feelings beyond the conception of any, save those whose bosoms have burned with a "lava flood" like that of my own.'

Two contemporary versions of what happened next differ somewhat, though the outcome for the tragic Mangan was the same. The lady having apparently encouraged him, turned him away. John Mitchel, who knew him reasonably well, and was very friendly with many of his friends, charges Miss Stackpoole with being a heartless coquette who wanted only another trophy for her collection. 'Paradise opened before him,' writes. Mitchel. 'The imaginative and passionate soul of a devoted boy bended in homage before an enchantress. She received it, was pleased with it, even encouraged and stimulated it, by various arts known to that class of persons, until she was fully and proudly conscious of her absolute power over one other noble and gifted nature—until she knew that she was the centre of the whole orbit of his being, and the light of his life—then with a cool surprise, as wondering that he could be guilty of such a foolish presumption, she exercised her undoubted prerogative and whistled him down the wind.'

James Price, however, who was his friend and fellow contributor to a Dublin journal, is not quite so hard on Miss Stackpoole, but recounts that Mangan had the misfortune to introduce her to a friend of his who supplanted him in her affections. Mangan himself gave that explanation in the magazine article already quoted, but it must be remembered that such writing is given a slant which will make it popular reading and does not have to be true in every detail. Price, however, maintains that this is substantially what happened, and that the presentiment of evil which the poet relates overwhelmed him on that fateful evening, was indeed justified by the outcome. 'I well remember,' wrote Mangan, 'that, on the very evening of the introduction, a presentiment of over-shadowing evil hung like a cloud above my spirit. I saw, as on the glass of a magic mirror, the form and character of the change that was about to be wrought upon the spirit of my dream. Those who are familiar with presentiments know that earlier or later they will be realised. So, alas! it was with me. Shape and verification were speedily given to the outlines of my vague imaginings.'

Poor Mangan, of course, in chronic ill-health from undereating, over-drinking, lack of any discipline, exercise, fresh air or relaxation, and fleeing, as he did from the contacts which forced living as against existing on him, was indeed familiar with forebodings of every kind, and in many cases went more than half way to meet any possible disaster which might befall

him. Moreover, all his written accounts of the events of his
unhappy life savour somewhat of a persecution complex. Gentle,
charming, winning, as he was, he was also honest enough to
know that much of the mental anguish from which he suffered
was brought upon himself. 'I felt, or fancied,' he wrote, 'that
between me and those who approached me no species of
sympathy could exist, and I shrank from communion with
them as from something alien to my nature. It was a morbid
product of pride and presumption which, almost hidden from
myself, constituted governing traits in my character, which
have so often rendered me repulsive in the eyes of others.'
Yet even with this much self-knowledge, he often ascribed his
failures and sufferings, when he came to write about them,
to the misjudgements of others.

Thus, a third version of his unhappy love affair, which he
confided to Charles Gavan Duffy, of *The Nation*, may well
contain more fact than either of the foregoing which were written
some time after its conclusion. 'This delightful and unhappy
man of genius,' says Gavan Duffy, 'has had his life made the
subject of strange and fantastic speculations, especially about
the event which made him an unhappy lover, which has been
accounted for on half a dozen theories, all of them wrong. As
the facts are familiar to me it is better, perhaps, that I should
state them here. Shortly after our acquaintance commenced,
he brought me to visit a County Clare family, a Mrs. Stackpoole
and her daughters. . . . I repeated that visit several times, always
in company with Mangan. One night, coming away, he suddenly
stopped in the moonlit street, and laying his hands on my
shoulders and looking into my face, demanded: "Isn't it true
that you are becoming attached to Margaret?" and finally he
said: "I shall save you from my fate by telling you a tragic
story. When I knew Margaret first I was greatly attracted by
her charming manners and vivid esprit. I talked to her of
everything I did and thought and hoped, and she listened as
willingly, it seemed, as Desdemona to the Moor. I am not a
self-confident man—far from it—but when I besought her to
be my wife I believed I was not asking in vain. What think
you I heard? That she was already two years a wife, and was

living under her maiden name till her husband returned from
an adventure which he had undertaken to improve their fortune."

' "You cannot think," I said, "that she deceived you intention-
ally, since you have not broken with her."

' "Ah," he said, "she has made my life desolate, but I cannot
help returning like the moth to the flame".'

What is one to think of this strange story, unless that it be
the truth? Mangan, moved by deep emotion, and possibly
also by fears for his friend, could hardly have composed such
a story on the spur of the moment in the street. Nor would
a man of Duffy's character later repeat and allow to be published
something he knew to be false. There is, of course, the very
possible explanation that Miss Stackpoole, having inadvertently
by her sympathetic interest in the poet's thoughts and dreams
led him to believe her in love with him, and being unwilling to
break his heart, rejected him with an excuse at once as gentle
as it was final. Yet, if she were unmarried, and very properly
entertaining young men in her mother's home with marriage
in view, would she have taken the risk first of Mangan's repeating,
as he did, the story that she was already married, and secondly,
of his finding out that she was not, if she were to marry one of
his circle of friends? The love story has a shadowy, half-unreal
quality, like the lover himself, and it has kept its secret for
over a hundred years. Whatever the cause of his rejection,
Mangan never recovered from the blow, and never looked at a
woman again. There are many references in his poetry and his
prose writings to the bitter lot of the unwanted lover, and the
Dublin University Magazine of 1839 contains a full length poem,
To Laura, which dwells entirely on this tragic subject, and is,
as Mitchel says, 'one of his dreariest songs of sorrow.' With a
verse of it we shall allow Mangan the last word.

> 'I sigh—where none my sighs return;
> I love—but am not loved again.
> Till life be past this heart must burn,
> With none to soothe or share its pain.'

Swift and Stella

A STRANGE AND INTRIGUING STORY, the history of the association between Jonathan Swift, Dean of St. Patrick's Cathedral, author of *Gulliver's Travels* and *Drapier's Letters*, and Hester Johnson, the lady immortalised in his correspondence as Stella. Like most of the haunting mysteries of human relationships which have fascinated people in all ages, it is one to which we are never likely to find the true solution, or to be sure that any one solution is indeed the truth. But that will never stop people from trying. It is plain to anyone who has read the *Journal to Stella* and knows the main facts of Swift's life, that the bond between Swift and Stella was very close. How close, what understanding, if any—or perhaps unspoken—lay between them, who gave the best part of a lifetime to each other—remains the mystery.

They first met when Hester Johnson was a little girl of eight and Swift a young man of twenty-two, in the household of Sir William Temple at Moor Park in Surrey. In 1688 Swift, then a young graduate of Trinity College, Dublin, visited his mother, whom he had not seen since early childhood, in Leicester. She, envisaging his situation with some dismay, prevailed upon him to get in touch with relations, the Temples, who were people of wealth and distinction. Sir William Temple was a diplomatist of international repute, who had arranged, among other things, the marriage between William of Orange and Mary, daughter of James II. He responded to Swift's approach and gave him a place in his household as a secretary. Also members of the household at this time were Dorothy, his wife, Lady Giffard his sister, and the little girl Hester Johnson. Her mother was a kind of housekeeper and Hester was one of three children. There is no doubt that a certain mystery is attached to her presence there. She was the only one of her family actually to live in Moor Park. Her mother, at the time of Swift's coming, was a widow, and has been described as an enigmatic person who had 'seen more of the world than might have been expected.' Sir William Temple entrusted Swift with Hester's education, a fairly unusual proceeding in the case of the housekeeper's daughter, and left her a substantial legacy at his death. She grew into a young woman of very considerable beauty, high intelligence and breeding superior to her origins. It was commonly believed during her lifetime and by many biographers since, that she was a natural daughter of Sir William Temple and Mrs. Johnson, though there are, in fact, as many grounds for disbelieving this as for accepting it. The one person who could have thrown light on it, Swift himself, is deliberately vague and misleading in his final account 'On the Death of Stella,' written the night she died. At any rate, there began in 1688 between the little girl and the moody genius who formed her mind an attachment which was to last until her death, forty years later.

It was a strange fate indeed that projected the charming little girl into the orbit of the great, sombre, tragic Dean of St. Patrick's: an irony worthy of the many bitter ironies which attended him from the cradle to the grave. A proud and haughty spirit, he began life with the handicap of being born seven months after the death of his father and was thereby dependent on relatives for an education and a start in life. Only the possessor of such an inborn, stubborn pride can fully realise the corrosion of spirit induced by subjection to the arbitrary will of people whose only claim to superiority is wealth and influence. A lighter temperament will accept the good in the situation, and even Swift was not always without gratitude; but it was his misfortune to be endued with a temperament in which the dark thread of resentment and bitterness predominated.

In 1694, impatient that his influential relative Sir William Temple had not shown his appreciation of his obvious brilliance by obtaining an entry for him into the Church of England, Swift left Moor Park and departed for Ireland, where he determined to make his own way in the Church of Ireland. There was a marked coolness in the relations between them and the

breach, though it was eventually healed, left a permanent mark
on Swift's character. Something inside him went a little sour.
He had thought highly of Temple and perhaps felt his trust
had been undervalued. Possibly he felt ungrateful and refused
to admit that the decision was a wrong one. At any rate he
felt the need of sympathy and affection and during his stay
in Ireland, between 1694 and 1700, he fell in love with a young
lady, the cousin of a fellow Churchman, named Jane Waring.
With his felicitous aptitude for pet names he called her Varina,
and to her he made his only known proposal of marriage. By
a man of his character such a proposal was not made lightly.
As a matter of fact he was in deadly earnest, and a reading of
his subsequent history in which he appears to have been moved
almost entirely by ambition, and bitterly angered when his
ambitions were thwarted, must be tempered by the realisation
that there were in his nature both ardour and idealism, which
later were savagely repressed.

Most tragically for Swift, and indeed for Stella, Varina seems
to have been a girl of lukewarm passion, greatly dominated by
her family who did not regard Swift as a matrimonial prize.
She did not break with him at once after his proposal, but to
his entreaties for her decision she made temporizing replies
which slowly killed his dream. During the period, Sir William
Temple offered him his post again with finer terms and far
greater prospects. To refuse him meant to end the possibility
of his patronage and all hope of a brilliant career in the Church
of England, which was very near to his heart. Yet he determined
that if Varina would marry him he would put aside that hope,
and be content to make his own way without help or influence
in Ireland. He wrote to her: 'I am once more offered to have
the same acquaintance with greatness that I formerly enjoyed,
and with better prospect of advantage. I here solemnly offer
to forego it all for your sake. . . . By heaven, Varina, you are
more experienced and have less of virgin innocence than I. . . .
Love, with the gall of too much discretion, is a thousand times
worse than with none at all. To resist the violence of our
inclinations at the beginning is a strain of self-denial that may
have some pretences to set up for a virtue; but when they are

grounded at first upon reason, when they have taken firm root
and grown up to a height, it is folly—folly as well as injustice,
to withstand their dictates . . . and it is as possible to err in
excess of piety as of love. These are the rules I have long
followed with you, Varina, and had you been pleased to imitate
them, we should both have been infinitely happy. Farewell,
Madam, ... Only remember that if you still refuse to be mine,
you will quickly lose, forever lose, him that is resolved to die
as he has lived, all yours.'

Varina, whether unaware of the totality of the offer, or
unwilling to reciprocate with such completeness, could not give
him the straight answer he required. He did not ask again.
He returned to Moor Park, though he did not immediately
resign his Irish living, where he undertook more important
and confidential work than before. And he met again Hester
Johnson, whom he christened Stella, now grown to be a quite
lovely young woman. She was then looked upon, as he wrote
of her many years later: 'as one of the most beautiful, graceful
and agreeable young women in London. . . . Her hair was blacker
than a raven, and every feature in perfection.'

In every man's life there are conflicts, disappointments,
turning-points. If the man is a genius, with the highly sensitised
perceptions and strong emotional reactions which usually
accompany genius, these inevitable reverses with their attendant
humiliation, may leave searing scars. By 1696 Swift had had
two serious reversals, and they had shattered his belief first
in man and next in woman. That he was mistaken to take these
blows to his pride with such deep-rooted hurt and bitterness
is unarguable. Like most ardent and idealistic natures he had
credited the objects of his affection with too many virtues.
Temple was a good and generous man, but not as completely
noble, not so godlike in stature as Swift imagined him to be.
Varina, a tender, possibly timid young woman, was not capable
of the consuming passion, the selfless abandonment for which
Swift had hoped. Cynicism, a quality previously foreign to
his nature, came to stay. It had not yet assumed the proportions
of the *saeva indignatio* which warped his later years, but it
became a part of the impregnable barrier of caution and calcul-

ation with which he now surrounded himself. He would not be made to suffer again.

In this unhappy, sterile frame of mind he was brought into close contact with the lovely blossoming Stella. Here was a young, unformed spirit, as yet unsullied by the knowledge of the falseness of mankind. He took up her education again, but this time with a different object in view. She could do all the things a normally literate person can do, and here now he found soil to plant the seeds of his newly acquired wisdom. He did not try to inculcate her with his cynicism, but he devoted himself to impressing on her mind the value of the principles of truth, integrity, loyalty, which he had found lacking in others. There is no doubt that he succeeded. Stella was an apt pupil, and devoted to her strange, brilliant, often humorous and always interesting tutor. In her eagerness to please him she became almost his alter ego, reflecting his influence to such an extent that their very handwriting became almost identical. But the tragedy of it was that the 'ideal' person on whom Stella was modelled, whom she was imitating and using as her criterion of all that was noblest and best in human nature, was not now a human being at all. The most important organ, without which there is no life, the heart, had been left out. Love, in any form, the mainspring of human action, the primary Commandment, was not a part of the education. That is not to say that Stella was as content with this standpoint as was her tutor. Indeed, from her very tractability, the opposite may be inferred. But whatever she felt for him at that time, he was determined that for her he would feel no more than the loving tenderness of the wise teacher for his favourite pupil.

In 1701, Swift accepted another living in Ireland, having resigned from the first in 1698. This was at Laracor in the diocese of Meath. Temple had died and for the time being it seemed that his fortunes lay in Ireland. The legacy which Temple had left to Stella was an estate in Ireland, and Swift used this circumstance as a means of persuasion to her to take up residence there. She probably needed very little persuasion, but in any case Swift, the cautious, had a good reason for his action if any criticism arose. She assented, and with a relative of the Temples, a Miss Rebecca Dingley, took up residence in Dublin. She was now twenty and he was thirty-three. It cannot have seemed too impossible that his friendship would in time ripen into love.

For the next few years the three of them, 'the ladies' and Swift, pursued a fairly peaceful, intimate existence. Swift crossed to and from England occasionally, intent as always on furthering his ambitions. He had now become something of a lion on the English political scene through his writings. Then there follows an episode which is perhaps the only one to throw any light on Stella's feelings.

A young clergyman of her acquaintance, the Rev. William Tisdall, expressed the desire to marry her, and got in touch with Swift as her protector and friend. At first Swift appeared to be very light-hearted and genial about the whole affair, and Tisdall was well received by Stella. Thinking the coast was clear, he now wrote asking Swift to help him by putting the proposal to Stella's mother, after the custom of the time. Swift's reply was in a different mood. He put difficulties in the way, and remarked on the disadvantages to Tisdall of an early marriage on a small income. Tisdall was discouraged, as we may presume Swift meant him to be, but the interesting point is that Stella, who up to this had been receiving him with favour, possibly growing tired of waiting for her unpredictable mentor, now refused Tisdall's offer of marriage. The conclusion which one must come to is that she judged Swift's discouragement of Tisdall as an indication that he wanted her for himself at last.

But life continued as before. 'The ladies' lived in intimate friendship with Swift, though never under the same roof, except at the house parties of friends. They did not even see him every day, but there is no doubt that he was the centre of their world. He continued to come and go between Dublin and London. His writings were bringing him fame though no fortune. He was now an impressive figure in the most exalted London political circles. And his personal life had begun to assume the rigidity, the negative, horrid logic of the man who has conquered his natural self for the most unnatural of reasons. How could Stella, equipped only with the weapons he had given her, hope

to pierce this armour? She did not, but one woman, unfortunately
for herself, though perhaps happily for Swift, very nearly did.

In 1707, during one of his journeys to England he met a
young lady named Esther Vanhomrigh, charmingly nicknamed
by him Vanessa. Her mother, the widow of one of the Williamite
officers with estates in Ireland, moved in his social circle in
London, and they met frequently. There is no doubt whatever
that Vanessa fell in love with Swift with the same abandonment
which he had given and looked for from Varina. She was young,
beautiful and passionate, and she stirred in Swift something
which the tender devotion, loyalty and love of Stella could not.
She disturbed the pattern of life he had laid down for himself,
and continued to do so until her early death in 1723. That
she imperilled Stella's position is very unlikely. He took the
attitude of the middle-aged clergyman to the eager girl with
her, and at no time ever indicated that there was any hope
for her of marriage. But though Vanessa was guilty of all the
indiscretions and excesses of any girl in love, he did not end
the association, embarrassing as it was at times, and it is apparent
from his letters to her that he derived great happiness
from it.

From 1710 to 1713, Swift was continuously in London,
and this is the period of the utterly delightful *Journal to Stella*.
Written at any moment he had leisure, and posted to her about
once a fortnight, it remains one of the most tender, teasing
documents in the English language, at once revealing and completely
veiling the writer and the recipient. That Swift deliberately
cloaked his relationship with Stella from the rest of the
world during his lifetime and in his account of her death for
posterity, is clear enough. But what becomes equally clear
from a reading of the *Journal* is that he was also deceiving
himself about his feelings towards her. It is a dilemma which
must eventually be faced by all who exert undue influence on
others. Swift deliberately made Stella what he wanted her to
be. And now what was that? And did he really want it?

In 1716 some crisis arose in their relationship. Swift was
now Dean of St. Patrick's, and bitterly chagrined at this culmination
of his ambitions. Vanessa had moved to her family's

estate in Celbridge to be near him. About this time Stella
wrote a poem *On Jealousy* which begins:

O shield me from his rage celestial Powers!
This tyrant that embitters all my hours.

It was firmly maintained by all their contemporaries, though
it has been alternatively denied and confirmed since, that Stella,
discovering the truth of Vanessa's love for Swift, was deeply
hurt and fell into bad health. The account continues that to
calm her fears of being deserted by him, Swift entered into a
marriage with her in name only, which was performed by a
personal friend, the Bishop of Clogher, in the garden of the
Deanery there. His conditions were that they should live as
before in separate establishments, and that the marriage should
be kept secret. Stella agreed to the conditions, for at least it
removed the fear of Vanessa.

Vanessa, it is certain, knew nothing of the marriage. Towards
1720, tuberculosis attacked her younger sister who lived with
her, and Vanessa herself in a few years contracted and died
of the same disease. Contemporary accounts state that she
discovered at this time the story of Swift's marriage to Stella,
and the blow hastened her end. Whether this is true it is
impossible to maintain, but on her death Swift left Dublin for a
prolonged journey around the South of Ireland, and was out
of touch with Stella for many months.

The story then takes an unexpected turn. A contemporary
source says that just before Vanessa's death, Swift proposed
to Stella that they live as man and wife, but that she refused
because 'the Dean's temper was so altered. . . . and her own health
at the same time gradually impaired.' The following year
he became ill and she nursed him with great devotion, but after
that she fell into real ill-health from which she never recovered.
The years 1726-1728 are for Swift one long effort to escape
from the agony of watching Stella die. He went to London,
came back, went again and stayed, waiting for the final word,
but returned again to find her still clinging to life. In January,
1728, however, she died. Swift was with friends in the Deanery
when the news was brought to him, and with suppression of
his natural reactions which had now become second nature,

he made no comment until his guests departed several hours later.

Then he began the genuinely heart-broken but maddeningly repressed document *On the Death of Stella*. He could not bear to attend her funeral, and even moved his bedroom so that he should not see the lights in the Cathedral during the ceremony.

He deliberately destroyed all her letters to him, and never referred to her in his correspondence again. But after his death, many years later, there was found in his desk an envelope containing a lock of her hair. On the outside, in his handwriting, were the stark words: 'Only a woman's hair.'

Did Stella love and live in vain? No. That the object of her unwavering affection was a tormented, repressed and brilliant man was her tragedy. That she brought him so much of comfort, loyalty and peace was her overwhelming reward.

Lola Montez

LIKE THE PASSAGE of a stormy meteor, the career of Lola Montez, descendant of the Olivers of Castle Oliver, County Limerick, rises, flares brilliantly but briefly and falls to earth with the complete extinction of volcanic ash. It is said of her that she was born a century too late, for she was born to rule in the grand manner of Madame de Stael. There is no doubt that had she come a century later, she would have ruled in Hollywood.

Born in Limerick in 1818, she was the daughter of an Ensign Gilbert of the King's Own Scottish Borderers and a Miss Oliver of Castle Oliver, who claimed descent from a Spanish Grandee, Count de Montalvo. She was baptised Maria Dolores Eliza Rosanna, but the romantic Lola was her pet name from childhood. By 1822, her father's regiment had been moved to India, and Lola had commenced the long saga of wanderings which ended only with her death. The gorgeous panoply of the East, the gay and irresponsible social life and the scarcity of women which redoubled masculine attentions to the women there were, made an early impression on Lola. The death of her father from cholera was a temporary grief, assuaged by the re-marriage of her mother to a fellow-officer, Major Craigie, who seems to have been remarkably fond of his step-daughter. When the time came for her to be educated, he arranged for her to be looked after by his own relations in Scotland, and afterwards with friends in London.

During ten years' absence from India and her parents, Lola grew into an astonishingly lovely girl. Tall, deep-bosomed, slender-waisted, she had long slim legs and dainty little feet. Her hair was glossy black and her complexion creamy and blooming. The reports of her charms had reached the lonely male hearts in Calcutta and beyond, and her mother, not

31

unnaturally perhaps, had visions of a brilliant match for her.
Concentrating on the financial benefit to her only daughter
rather than on any marital bliss incidental to the union, she
selected from a competitive field a venerable and extremely
wealthy gentleman of sixty, as Lola's prospective husband.
Motivated by a desire to do well by her, she remembered, no
doubt, the struggle to live handsomely on an Ensign's pay,
and had surely forgotten what it was like to be a full-blooded
and romantic eighteen. Without consulting Lola, she arranged
the match and sailed for England to select a trousseau and return
with the bride-to-be. On the boat she met a Lieut. Thomas
James, whom, in the tradition of Indian Army wives, she
mothered and confided in. He too confided that he was engaged
to be married, and so in this atmosphere of mutual trust and
affection, she allowed him to accompany her to her first meeting
with Lola. She was delighted, and so was Lieut. James, to find
that reports of Lola's beauty had not been exaggerated.

There commenced then a buying spree for Lola, when her
mother, to her amazement, heaped lovely gowns, lingerie,
jewellery and hats on her in such profusion that Lola, whose
brains about matched her beauty, began to suspect some catch.
Her mother evaded her questions, but Lola extracted the little
plot from Lieut. James who seized the opportunity to declare
his undying love for her. Lola challenged her mother with the
intention of marrying her off to a rich man, old enough to be her
grandfather, and a tremendous quarrel ensued, during which
Lola refused utterly to have anything to do with the whole
arrangement. Mrs. Craigie remained unmoved, but Lola took
action. Lieut. James proposed a runaway match which she
promptly accepted. They fled to Ireland, for James was a native
of County Meath, but there they had to await parental consent,
for Lola was under age. Not surprisingly, this was not forth-
coming. Mrs. Craigie had lost a brilliant matrimonial prize,
a daughter and a pleasant male companion, and she was not
disposed to give her blessing to such an arrangement. However,
she realised eventually that to hold out would produce nothing
but complete disaster, and she gave in but refused to be present
at or sanction the wedding in any other way. The young couple

were married in County Meath in July, 1837, and Mrs. Craigie
returned with the melancholy news to India.

The marriage unfortunately was not a success. In her autobiography, Lola wrote of it in later years: 'Runaway matches,
like runaway horses, are almost sure to end in a smash up.'
Writing from experience, she probably realised, all too late,
that marriage with her elderly admirer might have provided
her with an early and wealthy widowhood, a station in life for
which Lola was designed by nature. For a while the young
couple returned to India, where they led the social life of the
period, but in 1841, during their stay with a similar young
couple, Lieut. and Mrs. Lomer, bored with Indian cantonment
life, Lola's husband and Mrs. Lomer livened things up by
eloping. At this, in her own words, 'little Lola wondered,
cried a little and laughed a good deal,' but apparently took no
steps to reclaim her husband and eventually decided to return
to England, encouraged by her mother who had not forgiven
her. Her stepfather again confided her to his relatives in Scotland,
and pressed a cheque for £1,000 into her hand as they parted at
the ship. But Lola never saw Scotland. A gay party on board
ship included a Mr. Lennox, who apparently succumbed as
many before and after to Lola's personality and loveliness.
Mistress of her fate for the first time, Lola saw more attractive
possibilities in London, and refused to accompany the Scottish
representative of the Craigies who arrived to meet her. She
remained in London, and so, it seems, did Mr. Lennox.

An elemental creature, swayed by passion, pride, anger or
love, Lola never condescended to subterfuge or furtive conniv-
ings, and it was not long before Lieut. James had heard of Mr.
Lennox and instituted proceedings for divorce, a subscriber
no doubt to the theory that the pot has a perfect right to call
the kettle black. The divorce granted was *a mensa et thoro*, or
simply a legal separation which did not permit either party
to remarry, though probably Lola, who ignored the entire
proceedings, was unaware of this. Ironically enough, both
Lieut. James and Mr. Lennox disappear at this juncture from
Lola's life and are never heard of again.

As a divorcee in the London of the period Lola was not

acceptable on the surface of elegant society, though there were certain courses of action open to her which could give her entry through unofficial doors. In our days of floodlights, café society and the Sunday papers, it is difficult to recapture the mysterious allure of the *demi-monde* which was now to be Lola's natural habitat. She could have taken the easy way of accepting the 'protection' of some wealthy man about town, but she was not like that. Wayward and impulsive as she was, Lola did follow her heart, and was never guilty of a purely cold-blooded plan of action to better her circumstances. She was possessed too of a haughty independence of spirit which is one of her chief attractions, and she chose the more difficult approach through a stage career. She studied at a famous dramatic school, but all efforts to reveal any talent failed, and she turned instead to dancing and took instructions from a Spanish teacher. Now the magnificent flamboyant Lola sails into her own, no longer as Mrs. James, ex-wife of an officer in the Indian service, but as Donna Lola Montez, straight from the Teatro Real at Seville.

Dressed in gay Spanish costume and clicking her castanets, she made a striking entrance on the first night at Her Majesty's Theatre in June of 1843. Unfortunately she was almost immediately recognised by a titled member of the audience who, for reasons of his own, decided to wreck her performance by announcing her identity and hissing. As far as London was concerned, Lola's career as a Spanish dancer was over. But it had only begun in the rest of the world.

With an indomitable spirit which would have done credit to the Irish and Spanish ancestry she acknowledged, Lola departed at once for the Continent, and passed through Belgium, Germany, Poland and finally Russia, where she claims, in her autobiography, to have been on terms of the most remarkable affability and equality with Czar Nicholas I. Most *demi-mondaines*, however, like the good Americans, eventually arrive at Paris. In the spring of 1845, when Lola arrived there, the intellectual and artistic life of the capital was thriving and brilliant, and Lola was well able to maintain a position for herself among such writers as Alexandre Dumas, the poet Méry, Théophile Gautier and others. Here she encountered what was probably the only real and lasting love of her life, a M. Dujarier, literary editor of a paper called *La Presse*. They both fell in love, and in Lola's version intended to marry, but tragically Dujarier was inveigled into a duel with an opponent greatly his superior, from a rival paper, and was killed, leaving Lola 20,000 francs in his will. She was very deeply moved by Dujarier's death, and many years later referred to it as an irreparable loss. She left Paris, and Dumas, who had admired her greatly, remarked that he was glad she had gone. 'She has the evil eye,' he said, 'and is sure to bring bad luck to any one who closely links his destiny with hers, for however short a time.'

Journeying south from Paris, she came to Munich, which was under the rule of King Louis of Bavaria, a well-known patron of the arts. By devious means she managed to obtain an audience with the king in order to ask his permission to dance at the Court Theatre. Louis was instantly captivated by her beauty, and though he granted the permission, he decided that to have Lola personally employed near him would be very desirable. He arranged for her to give him Spanish lessons, and the friendship thus encouraged, ripened and prospered between them. He conferred Bavarian naturalisation on her, the titles of Countess of Landsfeld and Baroness Rosenthal, and an annuity of 20,000 florins, and consulted her continuously on affairs of state.

Lola loved power even more than adulation. Her relationship with Louis is claimed on very good authority to have been platonic, and it is more than probable that this is true. She would have been supremely happy conferring with the monarch, as she did, every day when he visited the mansion he had had built for her, and asked her advice on state matters. The feast of reason and flow of soul which resulted, in the most luxurious surroundings, the soirées at which she reigned supreme, and the deference given to her probably intelligent but superficial opinions, were undoubtedly highly satisfying to this egotistical beauty who was so well fitted to turn her assets to such good account. But Lola personally, for she could be fiery-tempered and arrogant, and her position as royal favourite, aroused deep and powerful antagonisms. Warring factions supporting liberalism and extreme conservatism, dragged her into their maelstrom.

Early in 1848, just about eighteen months after her conquest of Louis, she was compelled by his own order to leave Munich forthwith. Curiously enough Louis himself was forced to abdicate a mere six weeks later, giving substance to Dumas' opinion that Lola brought disaster on those whose destinies became entwined with hers.

After a short sojourn in Switzerland, Lola decided to try her fortunes again in London. Here she met a rich and eligible young officer of the Life Guards, who proposed to her and Lola tired of her wanderings and longing for an establishment of her own, accepted. They were married at St. George's, Hanover Square and Lola prepared to settle comfortably into matrimonial security. But it was not to be; her husband's aunt, whose opinion of Lola as a suitable wife for her wealthy nephew was poor in the extreme, discovered the circumstances of Lola's divorce and promptly reported them to the authorities. Within a fortnight of her marriage, Lola found herself, probably innocently, on a charge of bigamy. Her defence of course was that she was divorced, and the prosecution had no case other than the wording of the divorce, for they could produce no evidence whatever about the whereabouts of Lieut. James. An adroit counsel could have made them look foolish and possibly blocked the case, but unfortunately for herself, Lola's advocate practically handed it over to them. The magistrate was obliged to institute a further enquiry and granted bail. The Countess of Landsfeld and her husband could not risk the possibility that Lieut. James was still alive, so forfeiting the bail, they departed for the Continent.

Given the chance to lead a normal life in the London society, to which the position as wife of a wealthy Guards Officer entitled her, Lola very likely would have been a brilliant success. Cast adrift again in Europe, however, with a doubt on the validity of the bond between herself and her husband, the possibility of the whole relationship breaking wide open was very high. Tempestuous, independent, and thwarted again in her ambition to reign in some domain she could call her own, Lola was becoming literally a *femme fatale*. Her association with the officer lasted only two years, and she was wandering again.

From now until her death, ten years later, Lola's career resembles the movie versions of the saloon queens who moved westward with the covered wagons a hundred years ago. She had all the characteristics for the part. Beautiful, fiery, a brilliant opportunist, generous to a fault with her money, equally ready with pistol or riding whip to defend herself or chastise an enemy, she passed in somewhat dusty glory through America, north and south and Mexico, even settling for a time in a log cabin at Grass Valley among the Sierra Nevada. Even here, however, the strange fate which seemed to stalk her, caught up with her again. Her home was burnt down in a fire in the township and Lola departed, this time for Australia, where she entertained in mining camps and engaged in prodigious quarrels with the Press.

She began to tire of places quickly and left for Europe and then America again rapidly. In 1857 she was appearing on the stage in New York, in an item among others, entitled *Lola in Bavaria*. But like so many who have tried to drink too deeply of life's experiences, satiety and boredom took hold of her. She turned next to spiritualism. Very soon she declared that the spirits instructed her to turn from the stage to the lecture platform, a career which she now undertook with as much verve as ever she gave to an undertaking.

This 'desperado in dimity' now set off again for a lecture tour in Ireland and England, arriving in Dublin in 1858. She appeared at the Round Room in Dublin Castle in December of that year and proved to be an interesting, and therefore highly profitable, curiosity, though once again she wrote indignantly to the Press, concerning certain references to her which appeared in the *Freeman*. Her tour of England was equally successful, and during this period she became increasingly interested in religion. She began to be overcome with remorse for the type of life she had led, and returned to America a prey to scruples and dejection. Soon after her arrival in New York she encountered by chance a friend of her girlhood, now married to a city business man. The couple seem to have interested themselves very kindly in her, providentially, for her health was indifferent and her mental outlook deeply clouded with a sense of guilt. She became convinced that she was going to die soon, and indeed her premonition was correct, for within a few months she was struck down by paralysis from which there was no cure. Her friends got her into hospital, visited her constantly and arranged for a clergyman to come and give her spiritual comfort. Of her he wrote later: 'If ever a repentant soul loathed past sin, I believe her's did.

'She was a woman of genius, highly accomplished, of more than usual attainments, and of great natural eloquence.'

Lola was only forty-two when she died at the Asteria Sanatorium, New York, in January 1861, having lived on the razor's edge almost since her teens. Of her it might be said she loved not wisely but too much.

John Mitchel and Jenny

'POOR JENNY,' wrote her husband, John Mitchel, 'she might as well have married a homeless Bedouin or Wandering Tartar.' The wives of heroes are very often called upon to be heroines. And as John Mitchel is rightly judged to be one of the greatest men that Ireland has ever produced, so indeed may his wife, Jenny, be considered one of the finest of our countrywomen.

Theirs was an adventurous story. From the very beginning, Jenny must have realised that she had fallen in love with an unusual man, whose spirit burned with a clear and lovely flame, which enriched life but could consume it too, for the noble spirit is incapable of compromise. They met when John was twenty-one and 'pretty Jenny Verner' sixteen. John at that time was a solicitor's apprentice in his home town, Newry, and Jenny was still going to school. At all times a man who acted on his convictions, John knew that he had fallen in love with the pretty little sixteen-year-old whom he had watched on her way to school, and persuaded his sister Matilda to introduce them. Jenny was immediately attracted, and not unnaturally, by the tall, distinguished, sensitive looking young man whose expressive face and characteristic gestures were the mirror of a vigorous, imaginative mind. After a few months they became secretly engaged. Jenny's father was a military officer and an important member of the Orange Institution, and it was evident that the penniless son of a Unitarian minister would hardly be welcomed as a prospective son-in-law. Then, to the dismay of the young lovers, Captain Verner suddenly announced that he was departing for France and taking Jenny with him. Instant action was called for, and characteristically John Mitchel took it.

Jenny's parents had begun to regard her friendship with Mitchel with some suspicion and disfavour, and so it was necessary to put them off their guard. Nor could he confide his intentions in his own parents, though he loved them deeply, and so John announced that he was going to Dublin for a few days, and left Newry on the Dublin stage. He turned back, however, and returned to Newry where Jenny slipped out to meet him, and they set off in a hired carriage to Warrenpoint. From the pier there they hired a small boat and were taken down Carlingford Lough to the route taken by the Belfast-Liverpool boat, where they intercepted it and were taken aboard as Lieutenant and Miss Johnson. It was Mitchel's intention that they should marry as soon as they reached Liverpool, but to their great disappointment they were informed that this would require a statutory residence of a few weeks. They discovered then that the residence required in Cheshire was only a few days, and they crossed the river and travelled to Chester, where they obtained lodgings again as brother and sister, Lieutenant and Miss Johnson. John was gravely disappointed and worried by the delay in their plans, for above all he did not wish to bring dishonour or reprobation upon his cherished Jenny.

They remained scrupulously in the public eye as much as possible, sightseeing in Chester and strolling through the streets, and returned to their lodgings only for meals and in the evening. Here John, who had a fine voice, would read to her, as a safe and entertaining pastime. They were thus engaged when a few days before they were free to be married they were discovered and forcibly returned to Newry by the very angry parents of Jenny Verner. Captain Verner rather vindictively had John Mitchel arrested for the abduction of his daughter, but the judge dismissed the charge, and John who had travelled back to Ireland and been held for some days in custody was released. Meanwhile the Captain, who had not quite completed his plans for the intended departure to France, removed Jenny from Newry and placed her with friends in some place unknown to her fiancé.

But the John Mitchel who was later to endure the contumely of partisan judges, the injustice of packed juries and the bitterness of transportation and exile, was not likely to be separated from his beloved Jenny, who he knew reciprocated his love, by the arbitrary dislike of her father. He set himself to discover where she was, and he succeeded. Entirely honourably he announced his intention of marrying Jenny to her guardians, and so impressed were they by his sincerity and earnestness that they not only consented but agreed to help him, and on February 3, 1837, John Mitchel and Jenny Verner became man and wife in the church of Drumcree in County Armagh. Strangely there is no record of how the fiery Captain Verner or his wife reacted to this bombshell, but the Mitchels took Jenny to their hearts at once and for life. She was a loving and lovable soul, and through the thirty-eight chequered years of her marriage, brought nothing but joy, comfort and support to her husband.

After a short honeymoon they set up house in Newry, where after completing the next three years of his apprenticeship, John was admitted a solicitor in 1840. He then entered into partnership with another solicitor who opened a branch office at Banbridge with Mitchel in charge, and accordingly the little family, numbering now two children, moved there. Still lovers, and the best of companions, John Mitchel and Jenny delighted in long country walks together, and the countryside in which they lived provided them with much wonderful natural beauty. 'All my life,' wrote Mitchel in the years to come, 'I have delighted in rivers, rivulets, rills, fierce torrents tearing their rocky beds, gliding, dimpled brooks kissing a daisied marge. The tinkle, or murmur, or deep-resounding roll, or raving roar of running water is of all sounds my ears ever hear now, the most homely.' The gracious sea and mountain scenery of County Down, with its happy memories of Jenny and their early married life, remained to refresh and sustain him in the dark days of imprisonment and exile.

Living near Banbridge was an old school friend of his, John Martin of Loughorne, who also was destined to play a heroic part in the fight to better the truly frightful conditions of the Irish peasant just over a century ago. The two men had many long and earnest talks together, yet what John Martin's sister, writing to Jenny many years later, remembers best was the humorous, kindly, family man. 'Do you remember,' she wrote, 'a special pudding you used to have, and how your husband would look so comical and grave over "our pudding and sauce"? And what endless gay talk the two men had over all that was being done and written in the world. . . . But when you and he and the children would come to Loughorne, it was a sight to see him stretched under the shadow of a big tree, with his boys tumbling over him. He loved the sun and sky, and to watch the lights and shadows over the old lawn; and as he played with his children he was the very type of a happy man.'

In the same year, 1840, during a visit to Belfast on legal business, John Mitchel met Charles Gavan Duffy. It was a fateful meeting for Mitchel, inasmuch as the pattern of patriotic devotion and self-sacrifice which his life developed was commenced by his introduction to the circle which founded *The Nation*. Yet a man of Mitchel's stature would have taken the course he did whatever the compass which set his first steps on the road. He made an immediate impression on Gavan Duffy, as being a man of vigour and independence of thought, with a breadth of view and vision which the country, cowed, degraded, almost dehumanised by appalling misgovernment since the Act of Union, sadly needed in her sons at the time. Duffy describes Mitchel: 'Well-made and with a face which was thoughtful and comely, though pensive, blue eyes, and masses of soft brown hair—a stray ringlet of which he had a habit of twining round his finger while he spoke—gave it, perhaps, too feminine a cast. He lived much alone, and this training had left the ordinary results; he was silent and retiring, slow to speak, and apt to deliver his opinions in a form which would be abrupt and dogmatic if it were not relieved by a pleasant smile. He was already happily married, and lived contentedly among his books, in a little village on the pastoral Bann.'

Through Duffy, Mitchel became acquainted with Thomas Davis, who influenced him profoundly in political thought. Through Davis' eloquence he agreed to join O'Connell's Repeal Association and began to contribute articles to *The Nation*. He also wrote a life of Red Hugh O'Neill for the *Library of Ireland* series which *The Nation* were now bringing out. Then in 1845, in his prime, Thomas Davis died, and Gavan Duffy invited John Mitchel to edit *The Nation* in his place. Jenny, with perhaps an intuitive knowledge of what the work was going to mean to them all, tried to dissuade him at first from accepting Duffy's offer. But Mitchel was weary of the law, in which he was brought daily into contact with the evil system which was ruining his country, and he believed with all his soul in the work which *The Nation* was doing in trying to resuscitate the spirit of manhood in the Irish race at home.

He plunged into the campaign of exposing English mis-government, while insisting that the solution lay in the hands of the Irish people themselves. But terrible years lay ahead. During those years of the potato famine, two million died of starvation, exposure, and famine fever in the midst of plenty, and there began that dreadful tide of emigration with its inevitable outcome which has been luring young men and women away from their homeland ever since. 'The Irish people,' wrote Mitchel, 'always half-starved, are expecting absolute famine day by day. . . . They behold their own wretched food melting in rottenness off the face of the earth; and they see heavy-laden ships, freighted with the yellow corn their own hands have sown and reaped, spreading all sail *for England*; they see it, and with every grain of that corn goes a heavy curse.' Through-out the years 1846 and 1847, as the potato blight appeared again, reports of horror upon horror reached the office of *The Nation* from all parts of the country; thousands dying on the streets of the towns, whole families shutting themselves up in their hovels and dying like rats in dreadful agonies, wholesale evictions on to the roadside followed by arrests for vagrancy or plunder of food, the flight of hundreds of thousands from the death-giving shores of Ireland, which was nevertheless producing bumper harvests of grain all this time, and the useless, belated and humiliating steps taken by officialdom to alleviate what had become a world-wide scandal. One of these, the 'model' soup kitchen opened in Dublin, roused him to fury. 'There, in the esplanade,' he wrote, 'before the Royal Barracks, was erected the national model soup-kitchen, gaily bedizened, laurelled, and bannered, and fair to see; and in and out, and all around, sauntered parties of our supercilious second-hand "better classes" of the castle offices—fed on superior rations at the people's expense—and bevies of fair dames, and military officers braided with public braid and padded with public padding; and there, too, were the pale and piteous ranks of model-paupers, broken tradesmen, ruined farmers, destitute sempstresses, ranged at a respectful distance till the genteel persons had duly inspected the arrangements and then marched by policemen to the place allotted them, where they were to feed on the meagre diet with *chained spoons*—to show the gentry how pauper spirit can be broken and pauper appetite can gulp down its bitter bread and its bitterer wrath and shame together. And all this time the genteel persons chatted and simpered as pleasantly as if the clothes they wore, and the carriages they drove in, were their own—and as if "Royal" barracks, castle, and soup-kitchen, were to last for ever.'

Mitchel became convinced now that only the complete destruction of British power in Ireland could save the Irish people. 'I had watched the progress of the famine policy of the Government,' he says, 'and could see nothing in it but a machinery, deliberately devised and skilfully worked, for the entire subjugation of the Island—the slaughter of portion of the people and the pauperisation of the rest.

'Therefore, I had come to the conclusion that the whole system ought to be met with resistance at every point, and the means for this would be extremely simple, namely a combination among the people to obstruct and render impossible the transport and shipment of Irish provisions; to refuse all aid to its removal; to destroy the highways; to prevent everyone, by intimidation, from daring to bid for grain and cattle if brought to auction under "distress"; in short, to offer a passive resistance universally; but occasionally, when opportunity served, to try the steel.' He preached this doctrine in the columns of *The Nation*, and Gavan Duffy became alarmed, for he was not prepared to face a charge of sedition. Accordingly, Mitchel, who did not wish to jeopardise Duffy's safety, resigned from *The Nation* accompanied by a very able and fearless young writer, Devin Reilly. A week later, on February 12, 1848, Mitchel's own paper, named the *United Irishman*, appeared, numbering among its contributors James Clarence Mangan.

So passionate and stirring were its appeals, so enormous its circulation and so powerful its influence, that the Government decided to act. There was no law by which Mitchel could be touched, so they invented one, a new law called treason-felony, which made it severely punishable to write, print or speak incitements to resistance against foreign aggression. Whigs and Tories dropped their differences and combined to pass the Bill through both Houses and on May 13, 1848, Mitchel was arrested under its clauses and refused bail, for his influence was so greatly feared.

He was found guilty of this new 'crime' by a jury 'openly and notoriously' packed and received the savage sentence of fourteen years' transportation. On May 27, 1848, he was, in his own words 'kidnapped, and carried off from Dublin in chains, as a convicted "Felon",' aboard the *Shearwater*, on the first lap of the weary journey across the world to Tasmania. He wrote in the *Jail Journal*, commenced that day, and still one of the finest pieces of prison literature ever written: 'At Charlemont Bridge, in Dublin this evening, there is a desolate house—my mother and sisters, who came up to town to see me (for the last time in case of the worst)—five little children, very dear to me, none of them old enough to understand the cruel blow that has fallen on them this day, and above all— above all—my wife.' He was thirty-two, Jenny twenty-six.

Transported at first to Bermuda, the moist tropical air brought on asthma which very nearly killed him, but he was eventually removed to South Africa, and after five months there, to Tasmania. Here, on 'ticket-of-leave,' in the company of his old friend, John Martin of Loughorne, Kevin Izod O'Doherty, Terence Bellew McManus and the other victims of the unfortunate ''48' rising who had all been transported after Mitchel, he began to find again the normalities of life which had been denied him in the convict hulk at Bermuda and the Cape. Friends worked hard on him to bring Jenny out. She was doing her utmost to join him. Much as he longed to, he had firmly put the thought away, considering it too much hardship, but at last the effect of visits to the homes of other convict settlers softened his resolve and he wrote in his *Journal* of 'how blessed a privilege it is to have a home.' On July 22, 1850, he wrote: 'I do so pine for something resembling a home—something that I could occasionally fancy a *real* home—that I have written this day to Newry, inviting all my household to the Antipodes. Pray God I have done right.'

After her husband's conviction as a 'felon' Jenny, in the due exercise of the 'law' was deprived of his property, even his books, and as far as the Government was concerned, she and her five children were officially left penniless and homeless. However, a public tribute was collected for them (a humiliation that galled Mitchel) and after settling up certain matters, Jenny and her children returned to Newry and stayed with John's mother. She had longed to join him in exile. She had wanted to come to him in Bermuda and in Cape Colony, and had waited for over twelve months while he overcame his prejudice against bringing her out to Tasmania. She lost no time, therefore, when he consented, and sailed from Liverpool with her five children in January of 1851. It took them five months to reach him. 'To-day,' he wrote in the *Journal*, 'I met my wife and family once more. These things cannot be described.'

They set about finding a suitable place to live and through the subscriptions of friends in Ireland and a specially organised fund raised among the Irish and Irish sympathisers in America, they were provided with enough money to buy a farm and to stock it with sheep and cattle. Mitchel gave four hours every day to the education of his children, and Jenny, learning to ride, accompanied him on horseback all around the lovely countryside. It was not a bad life, though the prison atmosphere which prevailed was ever present and as he wrote to friends: 'Disguise itself as it will, slavery is a bitter draught. If our position were even worse and our prospects blacker, I should still write in good spirits, for I have no intention of being *subdued*; but. . . . I do not like that either my friends or my enemies should be led to believe I made myself happy by getting kidnapped and chained.'

In January, 1853, Patrick Joseph Smyth, who had had to make his escape to America in '48 and had since devoted himself to helping the transportees to escape, arrived in Tasmania with funds from the Irish Directory in New York to effect John Mitchel's escape. It was settled that if the attempt succeeded, Jenny and her children would follow under Smyth's escort as soon as would be considered safe. Plans were made and remade and at length after two unsuccessful attempts, John parted from Jenny again and set off for the town of Bothwell, formally to surrender his 'ticket-of-leave' for his honour and pride would not allow him to break his contract. This, of course, placed considerable advantage with the authorities who, fully apprised of his design to escape, switched all the available police to the work of the manhunt and filled every port of embarkation. Mitchel was forced to go 'on the run' and began to feel very depressed both as to his chances of escape and the fate awaiting him if recaptured. 'I may never see my poor Jenny again,' he wrote to his mother. 'I may never live to give her a peaceful home in America, and it is a horrible thought. . . . for she has been a good and brave and affectionate wife.'

After six weeks of heart-breaking near misses and mistimings for Mitchel, and of agonising suspense for Jenny, arrangements were finally made to get him aboard a passenger brig, the *Emma*, which was bound for Sydney. Meanwhile, as such a long period had passed, Smyth considered it safe to try and get Jenny aboard too. He circulated the rumour that John had made good his escape and was now safely in the States, where Jenny was going to join him. Accordingly, Jenny and her family, now grown to six, embarked publicly at Hobart and were cleared by the authorities. The ship, like all ships and stage coaches since Mitchel's escape, was thoroughly searched and cleared, and left Hobart, by previous arrangement, after dark. Four miles outside the bay she stopped and a 'Mr. Wright' was put safely aboard. The Captain welcomed him and introduced him to the passengers in the salon. But one lady who had been up on deck in the dark watching his arrival did not meet him officially. John and Jenny were united again, but not for long. At Sydney the police came aboard again, and were tactfully handled by the captain. Mitchel described the little scene: 'Captain Brown, who is familiar with the chief officer, takes him at once down to the cabin, produces brandy and water, tells the official person some new anecdote of a jocose description, and so gets rid of him. Then he makes ready his own boat, and tells Mr. Wright that he is going to bring him ashore first. Mr. Wright nods a slight farewell to Nicaragua, Smyth and his other acquaintances among the passengers, but does not presume to address Mrs. Mitchel (not having been introduced to that lady), and drops into the boat.'

At Sydney, Mitchel went into hiding again, as 'Mr. Warren,' risking only one meeting with Jenny. It was decided that as there was no ship leaving at once for San Francisco, their destination, the safest thing was to get Mitchel out of Sydney and British jurisdiction on a ship which had accommodation for one and was bound for Honolulu. He left therefore on the *Orkney Lass* and Jenny was to follow under Smyth's direction, as soon as possible. The *Orkney Lass* was diligently searched for him outside of Sydney, but the police did not recognise 'Mr. Warren' and she sailed on. After three weeks she arrived at Tahiti and discharged her cargo, which took another three weeks, and eventually she pulled out on her way to Honolulu. But there was a dead calm and she had to remain in harbour. Next day, while she was awaiting a pilot, an American ship was sighted outside. She hove to and soon a boat was seen to put off from her and make for the *Orkney Lass*. Mitchel in some anxiety took a telescope to determine what new danger awaited him, and saw to his great delight that in the bow of the small boat there sat one of his own sons and Smyth. Overjoyed he realised that his ship had been recognised and followed by the American, *Julia Ann*, and he and Jenny had a rapturous reunion beneath the freedom of the Stars and Stripes. 'Here then,' he wrote, 'Mr. Blake, Mr. MacNamara, (two of his aliases), Mr. Wright and Mr. Warren have all become once more plain John Mitchel. I am surrounded by my family, all well; and we are away before a fine breeze for San Francisco.'

Friends endeavoured to persuade Mitchel to take up his profession of the law again in San Francisco, where the prospects were very good. But he preferred to go back to journalism, and went on to New York, where his mother, brother and sisters were now living. But at heart he was never at peace outside of Ireland. During the following years he farmed, he edited, contributed to and published several papers, supplemented his income by going on lecture tours, published the *Jail Journal* in book form, and various other works including his *History of Ireland* which became a standard work, and lived in New York, Tennessee, Washington, Richmond, New York again and Paris twice. He took a keen interest in American affairs, and was of course, a strong supporter of the South during the Civil War.

Here family tragedy struck him. Mitchel and Jenny, with their youngest son and three daughters were in Paris at the outbreak of the Civil War when news reached them that the two eldest boys, Johnny and James, had joined the Confederate Army. Mitchel became anxious to return to the States and take his place with his two sons, but due to the blockade, travel to the Southern States was difficult and dangerous. It was arranged then that two of the daughters would remain at school in Paris, and that Jenny and Billy, the youngest son, and Minnie, should travel to Ireland. Billy, however, insisted on returning to America with his father to join the Confederates. 'So there is another break-up of our household,' wrote Mitchel. 'When shall we be at rest? Two, trembling and saying their prayers in Ireland; two, passing anxious hours in the Paris convent; and two making ready to penetrate the Yankee blockade in disguise, and by way of New York.'

John and Billy arrived in New York, but to get to the Confederate States involved them in a series of escapes and near-arrests that compared only with Mitchel's adventures in Tasmania, but after six weeks of dodging and hiding they arrived in Richmond. Billy enlisted in the First Virginia Infantry, James's regiment, and Mitchel himself reported personally to Jefferson Davis, the President of the Confederacy. He was disqualified from full military service by bad eyesight, but he joined the Richmond City Guard and an Ambulance Corps, and was called on active duty in both of them. He also used his great literary and polemic talents in the Southern cause, editing two newspapers in Richmond, first the *Enquirer* and later the *Examiner*.

In the early summer of 1863 there came the sad news from Paris of the death of one of his daughters, Henrietta. 'It is the first break in our family of six children, and there are three more on "the rough edge of battle",' wrote Mitchel, and very shortly the 'rough edge of battle' carried away his youngest son. Billy, on leave, heard that his regiment had been moved to Pennsylvania, and he walked the whole distance of 150 miles from Richmond to catch up with it. But his regiment was walking to Gettysburg, and there within a few days of rejoining it, Billy was killed. It was a grave blow to his father, though he wrote with his usual spirit: 'He could not have fallen in better company, nor, as I think, in a better cause.' Soon after this his eldest son, John, who was the first foreign-born officer to receive a commission in the army of South Carolina, and was now a Captain, was cited with two other officers for conspicuous gallantry. Writing to congratulate him, John senior wrote: 'I had a letter lately from Ireland. . . . . Your mother and Minnie were well,' and very impatient to be brought out here.'

Actually Jenny was more determined about it than her husband realised. The loss of two of her children decided Jenny that distances of thousands of miles between her loved ones provided no life for any of them. She had had her fill of separations and suspense, and she made up her mind to bring the remainder of her scattered family together at once. Knowing of the severe shortages which the Yankee blockade had now imposed on the Confederate States, she purchased all she could afford of clothes and provisions, and despatched them in packing cases to Falmouth. She brought Isabel from Paris, and with Minnie they now courageously set off in the winter of 1863, in a blockade-runner, the *Vesta*. They arrived safely in Bermuda, but were sighted off the coast of North Carolina and fired on by Federal vessels. The *Vesta* continued gallantly on her way, though she was constantly under fire, and was hit several times, but when it seemed that they might make good their escape, they ran out of fuel. There was nothing for it but to burn up the supplies of bacon, of which they were carrying a cargo for the Confederate Army, and by thus keeping up steam they managed by dark to evade ten Federal ships in pursuit, and were heading for Cape Fear River, which was safely inside the Confederate zone.

Then unfortunately the captain and first mate decided to celebrate their successful adventure, and in the course of their rejoicings ran the *Vesta* aground. The captain, well under the weather himself, thought that they had foundered on Federal territory and ordered everyone off the *Vesta*, so that he might set fire to it. Jenny and her two daughters were obliged to spend the night, along with the other passengers, three men, shivering in the dark on a strip of sandy beach and watching all their personal possessions go up in flames. Bad as was the loss of their carefully provided food and clothing, Jenny lost in that conflagration all her husband's letters to her during his years of captivity and separation, and all his private papers. In the morning they discovered that they were not in Federal territory at all, but in a swamp forty miles from the nearest town. The men set out to find some sort of conveyance, and came back with a wagon in which they drove the forty miles of swamp road to Smithfield from where they went by ship to Wilmington. From there they sent a wire to John Mitchel announcing their unexpected arrival, and concluded the epic voyage by train to Richmond. Jenny had braved now not only the perils of the seas all around the world, but had even run the gauntlet of battle to be with her husband.

Reunited with his wife and family John Mitchel took a house and began to enjoy a real home again. Jenny and the girls joined the Ambulance Corps, prepared hospital supplies and cared for the wounded. In the summer of 1864 they suffered the tragic blow of their son John's death, who, so his commanding officer wrote to Mitchel, 'was killed by fragment of shell while in the faithful performance of his duty, as commanding officer of Fort Sumter. The shot that has removed him has deprived the country of one of its most valuable defenders.' Much to their relief James, their only living son, who was also in the Virginia Infantry, was appointed to a staff post in Richmond, and survived the war.

The defeat of the South in the Civil War saddened Mitchel

greatly, though he had, of course, seen its inevitability for some time. The ruined Confederacy had nothing to offer him as a livelihood, and so he went north again, to New York, and took on the editorship of the *Daily News*, in which he endeavoured to put the case for the South and to appeal against the spirit of vindictiveness which was possessing the victors. But the doctrine was unpopular, and feelings still too high. Friends warned him of the danger he ran in expressing these liberal sentiments so much in advance of the spirit of the times, but Mitchel had never compromised on truth and he could not trim his sails to suit the mood of the victors. No less a person than Ulysses Grant, incensed by the temerity of this Southern sympathiser, ordered his arrest, and once again John Mitchel found himself under lock and key, where he was kept without trial and in great hardship for four and a half months. Eventually the activities of the Fenians in America obtained his unconditional release, but the confinement and its rigours had broken his health.

For the remaining nine years of his life, John Mitchel travelled a good deal. Against his better judgment he joined the Fenian movement after his release and consented to go to Paris as their financial agent. From here he wrote to Jenny: 'I am a lonely wretch. Very little can give me pleasure except to hear about my own folk. I have been twice to a theatre since I came, and both times quitted it before the piece was finished. . . .' He also went on lecture tours to make a little money, for his financial situation was bad and he worried a great deal about the prospects for Jenny and the rest of the family. But his health was giving way and these gradually became too much for him. Friends got to know, in spite of his efforts to conceal it, that the family were in poor circumstances, and a 'testimonial movement' was started, to his own annoyance and humiliation, which in a very short time brought to him the sum of ten thousand dollars. In these years he was often found standing in front of a map of Ireland, twining the lock of hair as was his habit, and tracing journeys across the country from north to south and east to west. 'An exile in my circumstances,' he had said, 'is a branch cut from a tree; it is dead and has but an affection-of life.' Finally in 1874, in spite of enfeebled health and the fear that the British might try to re-arrest him, he decided to take the risk of paying a visit to his native country.

During the twenty-six years of Mitchel's exile, much had happened in Ireland, but his own reputation and stature had, if possible, increased. Tremendous demonstrations greeted him, and the Castle authorities, who had had to make a law to arrest him, would have had to make another law to re-arrest him. They decided in view of the feeling in the country, and Mitchel's world-wide renown, that discretion was the better part of valour, and left him alone. He had brought his daughter Isabel, who had never seen Ireland, and together they visited Killarney, and he spent some time moving through the scenes of his childhood, his courtship of Jenny and their early married years, and returned to New York refreshed in spirit and somewhat improved in health. Jenny was very happy to see him a little better, but he was a prematurely aged and delicate man now. Early in 1875 he was asked to stand as a candidate for a seat in Tipperary which had become vacant. He agreed on condition that he would not take up his place in the British House of Commons. In February he decided to return to Ireland to conduct his campaign himself. Jenny was to go with him, but at the last moment it was decided that his son James would be of considerable use to help with the rigours of campaigning, and Jenny was persuaded by the other members of the family to agree to this arrangement.

The hardships of public meetings, wildly enthusiastic and heart-warming though they were, and the need to travel to different parts of the country were altogether too much for his failing strength, and when the day of the election arrived he was too ill to leave his room in the house of his sister in Newry, where he had gone to rest and recover. The result of the election, an overwhelming victory, was conveyed to him by telegram. 'How pleased Jenny will be to hear this,' he said when he heard the news. 'How pleased my poor wife will be!' The writing of a letter to his constituents was left to his brother William, for he was now much too ill, and realising that his condition was very weak he sent James back to America to look after the family, with a promise to Jenny that he would return at the first moment possible. The family, however, let Jenny know that he was actually dying, and she made arrangements to start at once for Ireland. But Mitchel's remaining store of strength was almost exhausted, and on March 20, as Jenny was about to set off from New York to join him, he died quietly in his sister's home. Of poor Jenny sacrifices were asked to the very last. After her many brave journeyings to be with him it was a heavy blow to be separated from him at the moment of his death.

John Mitchel belongs to the immortals. The incorruptible nobility of his mind and the gentleness of his disposition, his unbending hatred of oppression and refusal to come to terms with his enemy and his loving tenderness for his wife and children, the intensely human quality of his emotions coupled with the stern implacability of judgment which demanded such superhuman sacrifices of him, bespeak a character of the lofty proportions of a Washington or a Sobieski. 'Mitchel,' says Patrick Pearse of him, 'was of the stuff of which the great prophets and ecstatics have been made. He did really hold converse with God; he did really deliver God's word to man, delivered it fiery tongued.' Such an iron resolve, such an unbreakable spirit, could have ripened into bitterness as many have done before. But his heart was softened and his soul kept unwarped throughout a lifetime of disappointments and turmoil by the faithful devotion of his beloved Jenny.

Lord Edward and Pamela

On a fine November night in the revolutionary Paris of 1792, a distinguished French party took a box at the Feydeau Theatre, to hear an operetta by Cherubini. They were Princess Adelaide of Orleans, daughter of Philippe, Duke of Orleans, a first cousin of the imprisoned Louis XVI, her tutor and chaperon, Madame la Comtesse de Genlis, and a young girl of quite unusual beauty about whose origin there was some mystery, but who was known as Pamela Seymour. By a coincidence the neighbouring box was occupied by Lord Edward Fitzgerald, who was staying in Paris at the time, a deeply interested onlooker at the progress of the Revolution.

Lord Edward, who was then twenty-nine and heart free after one or two earlier unsuccessful love affairs, was instantly captivated by the lovely stranger. His companion, Hurford Stone, was acquainted with Madame la Comtesse, and arranged an introduction after the performance. As Madame and the two young ladies were leaving Paris next day for the less turbulent atmosphere of Belgium there was not much time to pursue the acquaintance. However, Madame de Genlis was impressed with the young man's obvious interest in Pamela and more than willing to encourage it, so she invited him to dinner with them the following evening at Rancy where they would be staying en route for Tournai. Lord Edward accepted with alacrity. He was already more than half in love, for he found that Pamela's manner and personality were as graceful and winning as her looks. To Pamela he must have appeared a Prince Charming indeed. He was very gracious, attractive if not exactly handsome, generous, enthusiastic and of good family. Small wonder that when Edward, with characteristic impetuosity, proposed to her after dinner at Rancy, she accepted him with equal eagerness.

55

Love at first sight is often the subject of sceptical utterances and cynical prophecies, but of course what the cynics, and withal inexpertly, are discussing is infatuation. Love, which is a facet of truth, sees clearly and feels instinctively and deeply. Beneath Pamela's lovely form and gracious bearing Edward quite rightly discerned sympathy and understanding. Behind the attractions of an Anglo-Irish nobleman, an apparently excellent matrimonial prize, Pamela perceived the complete goodness, integrity, generosity and warmth of Edward's loving and lovable nature.

Though apparently from very different worlds, Edward and Pamela had much in common. While Edward was the son of one of the oldest titled families in Ireland, possessed of great power and influence, even at the level of the English court, he was still a younger son. For this reason he was not precisely what the hostesses of Dublin and London society sought for their daughters. Pamela, while moving in exalted French circles, was in a somewhat similar position. There seems conclusive evidence that she was in fact the natural daughter of the Duke of Orleans, and her tutor, Madame la Comtesse de Genlis. Thus, while her parentage was aristocratic, her manners correct and her background semi-royal, the irregularity of her birth was a deterrent to marrying well.

Both had had set-backs and unhappinesses in their lives. Pamela had had, indeed, a strange upbringing. Madame la Comtesse de Genlis, a worldly and ambitious woman of high intelligence, had entered the service of the Duke of Orleans as tutor to his children when she was twenty-four. Her life as the wife of the Comte de Genlis had proved altogether too uneventful for her, and she was determined to obtain a position of influence in the court circles of France. Her absence from the Duke's court for a period of some months in 1776, would seem to have been the occasion of the birth of her daughter, but Pamela did not make her appearance in France until she was twelve years old. During all that time she was brought up in the village of Christchurch in Hampshire by a young woman called Mary Sims. One day a French gentleman arrived in the village; he happened to be the Duke of Orleans' horse-agent; and left with Pamela in his charge. The explanation given by the Countess for the appearance at the Palais Royal of the charming little girl was that she had been charged by the Duke to find a suitable companion for his daughter. The story does not seem to have convinced anyone, but Pamela was introduced to French society as the adopted daughter of Madame de Genlis. Such a violent change cannot but have contributed to a sense of insecurity in the child, and life at the Palais Royal was hardly less confusing. Philippe Egalité, as he entitled himself at the outset of the Revolution, was constantly intriguing with the Revolutionary leaders, and had ambitions for the constitutional crown which he hoped would be the outcome of the upheaval. Pamela's girlhood was passed in an atmosphere of tension, conspiracy and not infrequently danger.

Edward had a more secure and affectionate upbringing, being the darling of a large and very devoted family. Yet, by the time he met Pamela at the Opera he had been, to a certain extent, rejected by the society of which his family was such an integral part. Socially, as we have seen, he was not entirely without drawbacks. His love for his cousin, Lady Georgina Lennox, was peremptorily rejected by her father on financial grounds. Politically allying himself with Grattan and Curran he gradually became *persona non grata*. A man of eager sympathies, kind heart and vivid imagination, he was appalled by the wretched condition of the country from which his family drew their wealth and lived their lives of extravagant luxury in the midst of starvation and despair. He became a member of the Irish Parliament, as was expected of a man in his position, but he could not support the Government which entrenched its position behind the Penal Laws and Coercion Acts designed to ground out utterly a subjugated and bitter people. His chief interest lay in military matters, in which he was very talented. In 1789, through family influence, the chance of excellent promotion, with a brilliant future, was held out to him, adroitly laced with the suggestion that the man who held such a favoured command would not be expected to continue in opposition to His Majesty's Government, as represented in Ireland by the hated Fitzgibbon and the Castle coterie. With the integrity which distinguishes Edward Fitzgerald as one of the noblest characters on the canvas

of Irish history, he refused the enticement, and in doing so
put himself forever outside the magic circle. In the language
of today, he was thenceforward classified as 'politically unreliable'
and bore all the disadvantages that go with that category. Even
the most influential members of his immensely powerful family
could do nothing for him then; or dare not.

He struck up a deep friendship with Thomas Paine, author
of the *Rights of Man*, and interested himself in the doctrines of
social justice and political freedom in general, with particular
reference in his own mind to the cynical annihilation of such
ideals in his own country. Naturally the development of the
French Revolution held much to absorb him, and it was while
he was staying with Paine in Paris that Pamela so suddenly
entered his life.

When Madame de Genlis was informed of Edward's proposal,
though she was very pleased at the prospect of such a suitable
match for her daughter, she suggested that he obtain the consent
of his mother, the Duchess of Leinster. Edward left immediately
for England. It was late November, and he wished to be married
before Christmas. The Duchess was a wise and affectionate
woman. She knew what his political views had cost her son,
and believed that a happy marriage might give the anchorage
to his unsettled spirit. Her approval assured, preparations went
ahead, and Edward and Pamela were married on December 27,
1792. Among the witnesses were Philippe Egalité, Duke of
Orleans, and Louis Philippe Egalité, later to be Louis Philippe,
the Citizen King of France.

There commenced now for Lord Edward a period of the
deepest domestic and personal happiness. He had been quite
right in his choice. In fact, looking at the course of his life,
it is impossible to imagine him married to any of the conventional
debutantes of his time, with all the weight of their family power
and interference behind them. Pamela was .gay, charming,
sociable, but she was also compliant and understanding. Edward's
family loved her. Immediately after their marriage they spent
three weeks in London with his mother, and crossed to Ireland
early in the New Year. They had no home of their own at the
time, but they were welcome guests with Edward's brother,

the Duke of Leinster, both in Leinster House and at Carton in County Wicklow, and spent much time with other relatives in and around Dublin.

In April they moved to Frescati, his mother's lovely villa at Monkstown, which they were to use as a temporary home until they found something suitable. There is an idyllic quality about their life here for the next twelve months. Pamela was expecting a baby and was out of the social whirl, which she loved, for a while. Edward, never an enthusiastic socialite, but an extremely keen and talented gardener, spent his time beautifying his garden and growing plants for indoors, and in general being the young squire with his delightful wife. A year later, in 1794, they had the happiness of obtaining a home really of their own; a small but well situated lodge, set in its own grounds, in the town of Kildare, with the Curragh stretching from their back door. Their baby was a son, called after his father, and Edward's family life was complete.

The political cloud, however, still attached to his name, and his marriage to Pamela, far from dispersing had intensified it. Everyone knew that Pamela had been educated by Madame de Genlis, a disciple of Rousseau. She had been living in Paris during some of the most-violent phases of the Revolution; her home had been the meeting place of the best known Revolutionary leaders. Worst of all, her father, the Duke, had voted in favour of regicide. And Edward was a close personal friend of Thomas Paine. Pamela was not popular with the *jeunesse dorée* of Dublin, or rather with the female half of it. Lady Sophia Fitzgerald, one of Edward's sisters, says quite frankly that this was due to jealousy, for she was more beautiful than any of them, and although such a rank outsider, had married one of their society's most charming bachelors. Consequently as a couple who did not fit the conventional pattern, they were the victims of many wild rumours. Pamela was supposed to have a handkerchief dipped in the blood of a guillotined aristocrat; Edward was said to have taken to wearing a green cravat at her instigation. Some of this annoyed Edward. He wrote to his mother: 'My differing so very much in opinion with the people that one is unavoidably obliged to live with here, does not add much. . . .

to the agreeableness of Dublin Society. But I. . . . do not talk much on the subject, and when I do, I am very cool. . . . Yet all my prudence does not hinder all sorts of stories being made about both my wife and me.'

Yet they managed to live a delightful life in Kildare. Pamela loved dancing, and so they took many jaunts into Dublin to the season's balls and parties. Visits to and from relations filled happy weeks, and there were long walks over the Curragh, with Irish music and dancing in the evening. But the shadows were lengthening. Happily married, his simple tastes well catered for, Lord Edward might well have been expected to turn his back on the burning questions of the day. But the incorruptible love of justice, and compassion for the oppressed which detached him equally from blandishments or ostracism turned his eyes now to the desperate efforts being made to free Ireland from the stranglehold of the ascendancy. In 1796 he joined the United Irishmen and in May of that year travelled with Pamela to Hamburg, ostensibly on a visit to Madame de Genlis, but in fact, with another member of the organisation, to interest the French in a plan to invade Ireland and support an armed rising there.

Unfortunately, as we now know, every move of the United Irishmen was known to Dublin Castle, and Pamela was personally warned by no less a personage than the Duke of York that her husband was fishing in very troubled waters and in danger of putting himself on a charge of treason. Pamela's reaction to this information is unrecorded, but one must assume that her attitude was one of sympathy and tolerance. There is no evidence that she ever attempted to divert her beloved husband from the path he had chosen.

The Castle began to look upon Edward in a different light. Previously he was regarded as a disaffected but comparatively harmless hot-head. Now, an important officer of the United Irishmen, holding meetings at his house and in touch with other branches throughout the country, he appeared a more formidable opponent. Their spies reported that he would probably be appointed commander-in-chief of the projected armed rising. Two attempts were made by his family to persuade him to leave the country while there was yet time, but again there is no record that Pamela ever added her voice to theirs. In the election of 1797, he decided not to stand again for Parliament, and instead sent out an address to his constituency which plainly showed his hand: 'I shall not,' he stated, 'offer myself at present a candidate, feeling that, under present circumstances, there can be no free election in Ireland. . . . What is to be expected from a parliament returned under martial law?'

In the spring of 1798, the Castle decided to swoop, and with the aid of an informer, picked up the entire Leinster Directory of the United Irishmen in a house in Dublin. The spy, in some moment of remorse, warned Lord Edward, who did not appear, but a warrant was issued for his arrest. He went into hiding, and Pamela, who was expecting their third child and had been staying at Leinster House, left it and took a furnished house in Denzil Street. Here, worried by reports that she was being persecuted by the authorities, and ordered to leave the country, he made his way one evening in disguise. The shock of seeing him so suddenly, coupled with all the worry of his impending arrest and possible execution for treason, brought on her confinement prematurely.

From the beginning of March until the middle of May, he lived as a fugitive, hiding during the day and coming out at night for air and exercise. His health began to suffer under the strain, and now the Castle offered £1,000 reward for his capture. This was too much for the venality of an informer who, though Edward moved constantly, at last tracked him down to a certain house and sent a raiding party there. He was lying down when the raiders entered, but he put up a tremendous fight, fatally wounding one man and severely injuring another. He was overpowered, of course, and badly hurt himself. The Castle would have held him as a political prisoner, but the civil authority on the grounds of resisting arrest, had him moved to Newgate. His only message to the Secretary was that the news should be broken gently to Pamela.

Pamela hoped to be allowed to live in the prison with him, according to the custom of the time, but here the Castle was quite adamant, in spite of all the influence of the Fitzgerald clan, in their refusal to allow any visitors whatever. A few days after his arrest they ordered Pamela to leave the country. The Fitzgeralds advised her to do so, hoping that her compliance might make things more favourable for Edward. The prospect before him was grim, for not only was he almost sure of a treason charge, but probably one of murder too.

Yet the satisfaction of convicting him of either charge was to be denied the Castle, for his wounds were more severe than was at first realised and he became seriously ill. Not even when it was obvious that he was dying would the authorities unbend and allow him the comfort of his family. At last, on June 3, the prison doctor sent a message to his aunt to try desperate means, for he had not much longer to live. She made a frantic appeal to Fitzgibbon, who yielded and conveyed her with his brother to the cell himself. They were shocked to find him in an almost semi-conscious condition, though he had lucid intervals during which he asked anxiously after Pamela and the children, now far away in England. They were removed at midnight, and two hours later, Edward, the most affectionate of husbands and devoted of sons died, quite alone, leaving a widow of twenty-two and three children.

Two men in Irish history have especially endeared themselves to the people of the country. Both were young, both honourable and incorruptible, both brave. But above all, both are linked forever with the women who won their love and who were destined to be parted from them so tragically early. One was Lord Edward Fitzgerald, the other, Robert Emmet.

In the tragically unfulfilled love of Robert Emmet and Sarah Curran, poets and writers have found a fruitful theme for inspired writing, but who shall say that the love story of Lord Edward and Pamela, which bade fair to follow the pattern of the fairy tale of Prince Charming and his bride only to be cruelly robbed of its happy ending, was not in all truth the more poignant and pathetic one.

Richard Brinsley Sheridan and
Miss Linley of Bath

FOR A thoroughly delightful swashbuckling, gay and innocent
romance, the love story of Richard Brinsley Sheridan and Miss
Elizabeth Linley of Bath offers one of the most enchanting
examples in history. The facts of it arc as highly-coloured
as the most improbable fiction, and it possesses besides a charming
element of lofty chivalry, so unusual that it might even be
considered naive by our disenchanted modern eyes; was indeed
so looked upon for a time in their own day.

They met in Bath in 1770. Richard was then nineteen and
Elizabeth sixteen, and Bath was one of the most sociable, elegant
and stimulating places in the England of that period; teeming
with Royal patronage, artistic endeavour, intrigue, duels and
high living. Both derived from an artistic background, and
both were very talented; Sheridan, of course, was brilliant.
Born in Dublin in 1751, he was the grandson of Dr. Thomas
Sheridan, schoolmaster, and intimate friend of Swift and Stella,
and the son of Thomas Sheridan the actor and writer who wrote
an important life of Swift. In 1758 the family, who were in
constant financial difficulties, moved to London, where Thomas
Sheridan obtained a state pension of £200 per year to complete
an English Dictionary, much to Dr. Johnson's disgust! From
there they moved on to France, where Mrs. Sheridan, herself
the author of an excellent comedy, *The Discovery*, died, and
eventually they returned to England, settling in Bath. Richard
had been educated at Harrow, and was supposed to be taking
up the law, but in 1770, when they arrived in Bath, he had
commenced to write plays. His law studies were of very small
interest to him, but his good looks, charm and talents, brought

him almost too easily into the most polished circles of Bath's brilliant society.

Elizabeth Linley was the eldest of a family of five daughters and two sons. Her father, Thomas Linley, was a musician, a composer and a teacher of singing, very highly regarded in the musical world of his day. His children, especially Elizabeth and Polly, were talented musicians, and possessed voices of great power and beauty. 'A nest of nightingales' was how they were described by Fanny Burney's father, a doctor of music himself. But her talents, fine as they were, were far surpassed by her quite amazing beauty of face and figure. She was painted by Gainsborough when she was only fourteen, and later several times by Reynolds. She seems to have been as charming and sweet-tempered as she was talented and beautiful, and it is not surprising to note in Fanny Burney's Diaries: 'The whole town (London) seems distracted about her. Every other diversion is forsaken. Miss Linley alone engrosses all eyes, ears, hearts. . . . Her voice is soft, sweet, clear and affecting. She sings with good expression, and has great fancy and even taste in her cadences. . . . the best and most critical judges all pronounce her to be infinitely superior to *all* other English singers. The town in general give her preference to any other. To me her singing was extremely pleasing.'

Fanny Burney was so impressed that she made arrangements to meet Miss Linley in the Green Room after the performance, and of this pleasing encounter she reports: 'Had I been for my sins born of the male race, I should certainly have added one more to Miss Linley's train. She is really beautiful: her complexion a clear, lovely, animated brown, with a blooming colour on her cheeks; her nose that most elegant of shapes, Grecian; fine, luxurious, easy-sitting hair, a charming forehead, pretty mouth, and most bewitching eyes. With all this, her carriage is modest and unassuming, and her countenance indicates diffidence, and a strong desire of pleasing—a desire in which she can never be disappointed. I most sincerely and earnestly wish her well, safely and happily settled.' Fanny Burney adds here a rider which in view of Elizabeth's future was remarkably shrewd. 'I think,' she says, 'that so young a woman, gifted with such enchanting talents, and surrounded by so many admirers, who can preserve herself unconscious of her charms and diffident of her powers, has merit that entitles her to the strongest approbation, and I hope, to the greatest happiness—a union from affection with a man who deserves her.'

Amongst these throngs of admirers of the lovely Miss Linley, it would be strange indeed not to find the dashing Richard Brinsley Sheridan, but that Elizabeth should select from the many wealthy and well-placed gentlemen who swarmed around her a young, inexperienced and penniless playwright sheds an aura in the best tradition of romance over the whole affair.

As artists have discovered in every age, the admiration of the society which supports them is not always in proportion to its sincerity or integrity of purpose.. Elizabeth, for all her sweetness and youth, was launched in a hardened world. Her father, though affectionate, regarded her somewhat in the light of an investment from which he expected a return for all his time and skill in training her so expertly. Her beauty simply increased the public interest in her as a singer, and thereby enhanced his own reputation—and he had a large family to support. That she was pursued by the attentions of men who were not always desirable he was inclined to accept as the penalty of fame. That Elizabeth was innately shy, that for the most part she was afraid of, and indeed rather disliked men, he looked upon with good-humoured exasperation as childish and trivial.

In 1772 one of her least reputable admirers, a Captain Thomas Matthews, began to make himself a nuisance to her. .He was married and a good number of years older than her, but that did not prevent his amorous attentions. Though Elizabeth told her father and mother of her dislike and fear of him she could not get them to take her seriously. They thought her head had been turned by a few compliments and they made no effort to protect her from him, or to consider him in any way as a threat to her peace of mind. Had she been older she would probably have been able to get rid of him easily enough, for though persistent, he was not over intelligent. As it was, however, he frightened the life out of her with threats to tell all Bath that she was in love with him, or to shoot himself on her doorstep if she refused him, and various other tricks of his special trade. Poor Elizabeth was distracted. She could not imagine how to escape the dilemma, and in her terror and worry, she drank a bottle of laudanum belonging to her mother, thinking to kill herself. Fortunately the attempt was frustrated by the fact that there was not enough poison in the bottle, but it was obvious that she was prepared to go to desperate lengths to foil Matthews' unpleasant proposals.

Richard Sheridan and his brother, Charles, were now regular visitors to the Linley home, where their sister was having singing lessons. Both of them loved Elizabeth and she was friendly to them both impartially. But Richard's charming ways seem to have endeared him especially to her, and suddenly she confided in him the whole terrifying entanglement with Captain Matthews. Richard responded immediately and most chivalrously. Her obvious course, he suggested, was to elope at once. 'Elope?' said Elizabeth. 'With whom?' 'Naturally with me,' replied Richard. However, even her fear of the sinister Matthews did not drive Elizabeth to jump from the frying pan into the fire. She pointed out that she hardly knew him. Richard, fully aware of his unsuitability as a breadwinner, rose nobly to the situation, and explained that his proposal was purely platonic. They would elope, he said, to France, where he knew of a convent where his sister had been to school. For extra precaution they would take a 'duenna' with them, his father's servant and housekeeper. He assured Elizabeth that if she left all the arrangements to him he would carry them out satisfactorily and in such a way that her reputation would remain untarnished. In those 'Beau Brummel' days it was no light promise. It was an age of elopements and abductions, and very few of them were as innocent as Sheridan's genuinely was. Elizabeth trusted him and he arranged that on a particular night when Mr. and Mrs. Linley were to be out at a concert he would send a sedan chair to pick her up with her luggage. Then he was to meet her on the London road and they would travel by post-chaise to the coast. Where he got the money for all this organisation remains a mystery, but young gentlemen could do a lot on credit in those days, and there is a delightful record that his sister helped him 'out of the house expenses.' The plan worked without a hitch and while Mr. and Mrs. Linley were busy with their concert, and Captain Matthews presumably was hoping to use their absence for a rendezvous with his 'beloved,' Elizabeth, and her gallant protector, and the duenna, were bowling rapidly towards the sea. They crossed the Channel to Dunkirk and travelled on to the convent, where Elizabeth and the servant lodged, while Richard put up at the local inn.

No one at home had any idea as to where they had gone, and the consternation of the Linleys may well be imagined. Mr. Thomas Sheridan was in Dublin and knew nothing about it; and Charles, Richard's brother, was in the country. Bath was vastly intrigued. Elizabeth had so many admirers, but no one, not even his own brother, had ever considered Richard Brinsley Sheridan as the one on whom she would bestow her affections. Needless to say, Captain Matthews was furious. He inserted a ferocious paragraph, to which he signed his name, in a Bath newspaper: 'Mr. Richard Sheridan having attempted, in a letter left behind him for that purpose, to account for his scandalous method of running away from this place by insinuations derogatory to *my* character and that of a young lady innocent so far as relates to *me* or *my* knowledge; since which he has neither taken any notice of letters, or even informed his own family of the place where he has hid himself: I can no longer think he deserves the treatment of a gentleman, and therefore shall trouble myself no further about him than, in this public method, to post him as a Liar and treacherous Scoundrel.' One can visualise the delighted amusement of the pump rooms and card parties at this entertainment, which was as good as anything the theatre or the novels of the time had to offer.

Meanwhile Richard took a further quixotic step to safeguard his lady's honour. He informed her that he considered that they should go through a form of marriage together. He promised that he would make no claim upon her, and that when she returned to England he would consider her free to repudiate it altogether. It really was a completely noble gesture, and though Elizabeth was a little worried by the finality of it, her trust had been previously so handsomely rewarded that she agreed, and they were married in Calais, though no one knew of it then or for a long time after. True to his promise, he left France immediately and returned to England, while Elizabeth moved from the convent to the house of an English doctor and his wife in Lille.

The dramatic character of the story was not yet at an end. On Richard's return to England he sought out the fire-eating Captain Matthews, whose insolence immediately provoked a duel. A swaggering bully, he thought Sheridan an easy prey, but was dismayed to discover that he had been expertly trained by a professional swordsman. Consequently he did his best to avoid the engagement, but Sheridan refused, and after some angry scenes, they reached Matthews' lodgings where the duel took place in his bedroom. The whole episode is typical of the highly charged emotional quality of this love affair. Matthews, disarmed, refused at first but, at the point of death, grudgingly retracted his slander in the newspaper and apologised.

Elizabeth's father meanwhile discovered her whereabouts and set off for the Continent to bring her home. He was naturally greatly upset and very angry at the whole affair, which represented among other worries, a grave financial loss to him. However, his relief at finding that it had been carried out on such a lofty plane of chivalry and propriety was very considerable and he forgave the young pair, though he never approved of Sheridan. Nothing whatever was said about the secret marriage, and Elizabeth returned with him to her own home and carried on with her engagements as before.

Lest anyone imagine that there is a hint of anti-climax here, another duel between Sheridan and Matthews will correct the impression immediately. The news of the first duel with its humiliating consequences to Matthews soon leaked out in Bath and the fiery Captain was forced to issue another challenge to Elizabeth's protector. This time Matthews' sword broke and the two antagonists fell on each other, in a scuffle, Matthews continuing to strike at Sheridan with the broken weapon. They were separated eventually by their seconds, and Sheridan was carried home quite seriously wounded. The object of their bitter struggle was singing in Oxford at the time and knew nothing of the perils so handsomely encountered on her behalf by her gallant admirer.

Richard was nursed by his sister and then sent into the country to recuperate and to take up again his studies for the law, the profession still intended for him by his father. Thomas Sheridan who had returned from Ireland on hearing of the elopement was outraged. He disliked the Linleys heartily and was deeply affronted at his family's part in the notorious incident. He had no sympathy whatever for Richard's cause, not even for the honourable part he played in it, and hoped that by sending him well away from the fascinations of Bath and the proximity of the lovely Elizabeth he might forget the whole thing.

He was wrong. There was a reckless streak in Richard Brinsley Sheridan, which led him off into more than one adventure in his life. His volatile temperament often roused him to champion causes which he quickly forgot, but his devotion to Elizabeth was completely sincere and constant. Contemporary accounts say that early in 1773 Elizabeth went up to London to sing in Oratorio, and that Richard slipped away from his country retreat to see her. There were occasions when he disguised himself as the hackney coachman who picked her up from the theatre at night and drove her to her lodgings so that they might seize a hurried few moments together. She was, of course, always accompanied by her father, so that the trysts must have been agonisingly brief and dangerous, but the story goes that one night when the 'coachman' arrived she was alone. They made full use of their opportunity to arrange less hazardous and more congenial rendezvous, and eventually their parents, though still deeply opposed to the match, were forced to admit that the young lovers were undeniably devoted and obviously inseparable, so that further opposition would seem to be futile. The secret marriage was still a secret, though it had been a *fait accompli* for almost a year. However, they decided now to reveal it, more or less with the idea of forcing the consent of their reluctant parents, and almost twelve months to the day after the Calais wedding, they were married publicly in Marylebone Church, in April, 1773. Elizabeth was nineteen and Richard twenty-two.

It goes almost without saying, and it is only in keeping with the high-flown character of this romance, that they had no visible means of support when they married. Elizabeth was a trained singer, of course, with a very high earning capacity, but Richard magnificently refused all offers, even the most tempting, to allow her to appear in public again. The gesture is amusingly characteristic of him, especially in view of his own total lack of training for any livelihood, except his inborn genius, but it would seem to have carried Elizabeth's consent, for all her life she disliked singing in public. She had some money of her own, however, and he had immense faith in his creative talents as a writer.

In response to an invitation from the manager of Covent Garden, he wrote a play, *The Rivals*, which was produced there in January, 1775, and was a tremendous success. He also turned his attention to politics, and made use of his writing abilities on the Whig side. Then, as his name was now becoming widely known, he went straight into collaboration with his father-in-law, and together they produced the opera, *The Duenna*, in November, 1775. In 1776 he acquired the shares in Drury Lane Theatre of the great actor David Garrick, who was retiring, and these were a source of income to him, though neither then nor at any other time of his life did he manage to live within his means. Elizabeth worked even harder for him than she had for her father, copying manuscripts and keeping the accounts of the Theatre. They now had a young son; they were young, talented and popular, and Sheridan's social and domestic life was happy and complete. In May, 1777, his greatest work, *The School for Scandal*, was produced, and it is here, perhaps, at the flood-tide of his good fortune that we ought to leave him. His later life, largely due to the undisciplined impulsiveness of his own nature, which had been delightful at twenty but at forty was practically disastrous, was not entirely happy nor successful.

His love for Elizabeth, however, never altered, though when he became a public political figure, he was away from home more and more and saw her less and less. They had almost twenty years of somewhat chequered happiness together. Her love for and pride in him were unstinted and unfailing. She has left behind her the delicate fragrance of a gentle, affectionate personality, blessed with the twin fortunes of talent and beauty, and she was probably at all times satisfied with the somewhat spasmodic devotion of her quixotic and unreliable genius.

Lieutenant Close and Ann Grubb

ON A GREY March day in 1826 the body of a young officer of His Majesty's 86th Regiment, stationed at Clonmel, was found floating in the river Suir some little distance beyond the town. A few days later the river yielded the rest of its grim secret when the lovely form of his nineteen-year-old sweetheart, Miss Ann Grubb, was lifted from almost the same spot. A search which had been going on for them for three weeks was now dramatically ended. But though the lovers had been found at last, their tragic story has remained wrapped in mystery and silence to this day.

Ann Grubb was a beautiful Quaker girl, the niece of Joseph Grubb, an honoured member of the Society of Friends, who owned a prosperous silk shop in Clonmel. Ann lived with him, helping him to run his business, and was greatly sought after for her remarkable beauty. A contemporary writer describing her says: 'She was scarcely nineteen, tall, and notwithstanding the formality of her costume, the roundness of her arm and symmetry of her waist and bosom could not be concealed. Her eyes were hazel, with an expression of extreme gentleness. Her hair, Madonna-like, was parted on the forehead; but the silken cap could not hide the profusion of her silken tresses. 'Were anything wanted to make her irresistible, her voice was so musical, so modulated, that the listener held his breath to hear.'

To the numerous suitors who proposed marriage to her, however, Ann was courteously indifferent, for her love was already bestowed. Lieutenant Frederick Close, one would have thought, was an admirable choice in every way, for he had wealth, good looks and charm. His father was a wealthy Manchester businessman who would indeed have chosen a more prosperous career for his son than soldiering. But the

young man had spirit and when parental consent was not forth-
coming joined the army as a private. His father then realising
that his son meant business, purchased a commission for him.
In addition to his good looks Lieutenant Close was fit and
athletic, and for all that his life was so tragically ended, a fine
swimmer. But though he had every qualification for winning
a young girl's heart, his profession outweighed any of his assets
where the pacifist viewpoint of Mr. Joseph Grubb was concerned.
Not only did he disapprove of his niece's choice; he forbade
her to have any further communication with him.

But it takes more than an uncle's disapproval to alter the
course of true love. Ann and her young officer continued to
meet surreptitiously for months, and many stolen hours were
spent strolling in the shady old graveyard or along the banks
of the river. On a Sunday in February of 1826, they had arranged
to meet at eight o'clock. Though the evening turned out cold
and wet, Ann slipped away from her uncle's establishment just
a little before the time, and told only an elderly housekeeper
where she was going. The young lovers met, and were last
seen alive by some of the townspeople strolling down towards
their favourite walk along the river bank.

When Ann had not returned to her uncle's home at a very
late hour, the old housekeeper became uneasy and at length
decided to brave Mr. Grubb's wrath. She was obliged to add,
of course, that his niece had left to keep an appointment with her
forbidden lover. Grubb was angry and alarmed. He waited a
little longer and then put in an enquiry at the local barracks for
Lieutenant Close. To his consternation he learned that the
Lieutenant had not returned to barracks that night. Day succeeded
night, and no trace whatsoever of the young couple was forth-
coming. Enquiries sent out in all directions failed to produce
the slightest evidence of their whereabouts. One man reported
seeing a young pair enter the Fethard stagecoach, so Mr. Grubb
and an admirer of Ann's named Strangman, favoured by her
uncle, journeyed there. But no such couple had been seen.
The townspeople began to talk among themselves, and an ugly
rumour of foul play began to circulate. They had been seen
going towards the river, and the whisper went about that a

rival of Close, following them in the dark wet February night, had, in a fit of jealous rage, surprised them and hurled them into the flood.

Three weeks of anxiety and conjecture passed, until the discovery of the two bodies revealed their tragic fate. There was an inquest and the verdict of the magistrates was that no marks of violence were found upon the bodies, so that suspicion of murder could be ruled out. Nothing further could be done, but the people of Clonmel maintained their belief in foul play, observing that they had no motive for suicide, that the walk was in no way dangerous, and that Close was known to be a powerful swimmer.

Nine years went by, and in 1835 a Parliamentary election was held in Clonmel. The Tory candidate who was successful, was supported on his election committee by Strangman, the same who had been Ann's suitor and had accompanied her uncle to Fethard. After the election a series of articles entitled 'Sketches of the Late Election' appeared in the *Tipperary Free Press* over the pen-name of *Nemo*. They were unflattering in the extreme, as may be imagined, to the Conservative candidate and his supporters, and the pen portraits were so vividly written as to be instantly recognisable to the townspeople without mentioning a single name. The following extract from one of them caused a sensation in Clonmel:

'Pre-eminently officious was a tall, thin-faced young man (about thirty-eight), with light bushy whiskers, long nose, and a figure drooped at the shoulders, but not from age. What first fixed my attention on him was the unearthly excitement of his eye—it was terrible, such as no election feeling could conjure up. It was frenzied, and riveted me like a basilisk's. I asked my guide who the young man was, and his answer solved the enigma.

'I could not bear to look longer at his haggard brow, and with a chill I turned away.'

The enigma was that which had baffled the town for nine years, and at the sinister implications of the succeeding paragraph Strangman, for it was he, and all Clonmel knew it, decided to take action. *Nemo* went on:

'Years have flown into the ocean of eternity, and the winding Suir has emptied its bosom a thousand times into the British Channel, since the date of a fearful deed; yet the spirit of the stream still breathes two well-known names, and still the winter's blast howls over that fatal spot where those who loved "not wisely, but too well", met their melancholy, mysterious doom.'

The case, for libel damages of £2,000, of Strangman versus Hackett (owner of the *Tipperary Free Press*) was heard at the Kilkenny Summer Assizes. The action involved a review of the mysterious circumstances of the death of Miss Ann Grubb and Lieutenant Close, and this time there was revealed a fact which had certainly been suppressed at the inquest. There was a contusion on Close's head, so the magistrates said, when he was taken from the river, and the doctors who examined the bodies opened it, but reached no decisive conclusion.

Strangely enough the author of the article, *Nemo*, was not asked to appear in court. So significant was this omission that Hackett declared: 'The author, my Lord, would gladly stand forward, but they don't want him.' Did he know too much? There is no one now to answer that question.

Lieutenant Close is buried in St. Mary's Churchyard in Clonmel, and his lovely young sweetheart lies not far from him in the Quaker burial ground. If *Nemo*, or anyone else, knew enough to throw further light on the tragedy, he kept his counsel, but the belief remained in the town of Clonmel that on that dark, wet Sunday night of February 1826, a vengeful hand helped the lovers to their 'melancholy, mysterious doom'.

LOVE POEMS OF THE IRISH
Edited by Sean Lucy

This anthology shows those people who seem to think that we are a loveless race, how wrong they are. It takes a wide view of what can be called love poetry, a view which embraces a whole landscape of feeling between men and women, and does not confine itself to poems about being 'in love' in the more restricted meaning of that term.

IN MY FATHER'S TIME
Eamon Kelly

In My Father's Time invites us to a night of storytelling by Ireland's greatest and best-loved *seachaí* Eamon Kelly. These fascinating stories reveal many aspects of Irish peasant life and character. There are tales of country customs; matchmaking, courting, love; marriage and the dowry system; emigration, American wakes and returned emigrants. The stream of anecdotes never runs dry and the humour sparkles and illuminates the stories.

A HISTORY OF IRISH FAIRIES
Carolyn White

Whether you believe in fairies or not you cannot ignore them and here for the first time is *A History of Irish Fairies*. Having no stories directly from the fairies themselves, we must rely on descriptions by mortal men and women. A large part of the book is concerned with the relations between mortals and fairies, so that the reader may determine the best way to behave whenever he encounters fairies. The book contains such interesting details as the distinction and confusion between cluricaun and leprechaun and the fact that only male infants are stolen from the cradle. You can read of the Far Darrig, Merrows and Silkies, Banshees and Keening, the Lianhan Shee, Pookas, Dullahans and Ghosts.

FABLES AND LEGENDS OF IRELAND
Maureen Donegan

A fascinating collection of Ireland's favourite tales including 'The Pillow Talk of Ailill and Maeve', 'The Two Faces of Cuchulainn', 'The Voyage of Malduin', 'The Magic Cloak' and Oisin in Tir-Na-nOg.

THE MAN FROM CAPE CLEAR
Conchúr Ó Síocháin
Translated by Riobárd P. Breatnach.

Conchúr Ó Síocháin lived all his days on Cape Clear, the southern outpost of an old and deep-rooted civilisation. He lived as a farmer and as a fisherman and his story portrays the life of the island, (Fastnet Rock's nearest neighbour). He was a gifted man in many ways and developed great skills as a storyteller, a folklorist and a craftsman. The book is a collection of memories and musings, topography and tales, descriptions of old ways and crafts, and contains a fund of seafaring yarns and lore.

Hardbound.

MALACHI HORAN REMEMBERS
Dr G. Little

Malachi Horan Remembers is real and stirring history caught from living lips, just in time to save a hundred quaint, beautiful, precious things from oblivion. The book is a revelation. It describes authentically a purely Irish, robust, picturesque life, like that of unspoilt Donegal, Connacht or Kerry—thriving in the lifetime of the teller, on the hills that can be seen from Dublin's streets. Hedge schools, wooden ploughs drawn by bullock teams, fairy lore, quaint folktales, unique relics of Leinster Irish, road tolls—all are described by one who knew them. County Dublin, we see here, is truly an Irish-Ireland, too.

FOLKTALES OF THE IRISH COUNTRYSIDE
Kevin Danaher

A delightful collection of tales simply told and suitable for the whole family.

GENTLE PLACES AND SIMPLE THINGS
Kevin Danaher

These essays are about the beliefs and traditions of tinkers and highwaymen, of crickets and witchcraft, of fairies and ghosts; they are all here, and many more, treated with understanding and respect, but never with condescension.

IRISH COUNTRY PEOPLE
Kevin Danaher

Irish Country People is simply one fascinating glorious feast of folklore and interesting sidelights of history recorded without a fraction of a false note or a grain of sentimentality. The topics covered in the twenty essays range over a wide field of history, forklore, mythology and archaeology. There are discussion about cures, curses and charms; lords, labourers and wakes; names, games and ghosts; prayers and fairy tales.

IN IRELAND LONG AGO
Kevin Danaher

Kevin Danaher describes life in Ireland before the 'brave new world' crept into the quiet countryside. Or perhaps 'describe' is not the right word. He rather invites the reader to call on the elderly people at their homes, to listen to their tales and gossip and taste their food and drink; to step outside and marvel at their pots and pans, plough and flails; to meet a water diviner; to join a faction fight; hurry to a wedding and bow down in remembrance of the dead.

THE YEAR IN IRELAND—Irish Calendar Custom
Kevin Danaher

This beautiful book describes how the round of the year, with its cycle of festivals and seasonal work was observed in the Ireland of yesterday.
Hardbound & Illustrated.

IRISH FIRESIDE FOLKTALES
Patrick Kennedy

An intriguing collection of sixteen Irish tales handed down from generation to generation.

FOLKTALES OF IRISH FAIRIES AND WITCHES
Patrick Kennedy

A fascinating collection of tales and legends

THE FARM BY LOUGH GUR
Mary Carbery

This is the true story of a family who lived on a farm by Lough Gur, the Enchanted Lake, in Co. Limerick. The story is also a picture of manners and customs in a place so remote that religion had still to reckon with pagan survivals, where a fairy-doctor cured the landlord's bewitched cows, and a banshee comforted the dying with the music of harps and flutes.

THE TAILOR AND ANSTY
Eric Cross

The tailor and his wife lived in Co. Cork, yet the width of the world could barely contain his wealth of humour and fantasy. Marriages, inquests, matchmaking—everything is here.

ISLANDERS
Peadar O'Donnell

First published in 1927, the powerful novel depicts life in the early days of the 20th century of a small island community off the Donegal coast. This is the story of epic simplicity, of people who confront in their daily lives, hunger, poverty and death by drowning.

THE BOOK OF IRISH CURSES
Patrick C. Power

The Book of Irish Curses is an extremely interesting, well written, fascinating and entertaining book. It is a remarkable blend of history, folklore and anecdote. The author deals at length with the types of Irish curses, their age and styles, their rituals, and concludes with a do-it-yourself cursing kit.

THE FIRST BOOK OF MYTHS AND LEGENDS
Eoin Neeson

Fascinating tales from Ireland's misty past.

THE SECOND BOOK OF MYTHS AND LEGENDS
Eoin Neeson

A further collection of tales are contained in this follow up.

IRISH GHOST STORIES
Patrick Byrne

A collection of Ireland's most popular ghost stories.

THE SECOND BOOK OF IRISH GHOST STORIES
Patrick Byrne

As the author says in his introduction there seems to be an unending stream of tales of the supernatural in this country, and here are more uncanny tales.

IRISH GHOST STORIES OF LE FANU
Patrick Byrne

Urbane, witty and absolutely terrifying, these ghost stories are as much a pleasure to read today as they have been to his readers for more than a century since their original publication. The stories in this book, long out of print, are set in and around a bygone Dublin which Le Fanu so vividly evokes.

WITCHCRAFT IN IRELAND
Patrick Byrne

An enthralling history of witches and witchcraft in Ireland from earliest times ot the present day.

PYSCHIC PHENOMENA IN IRELAND
Shiela St Clair

Psychic Phenomena in Ireland is a unique blend of personal adventure and detailed research. It is a collection of 'ghoulies and ghosties and things that go bump in the night', and Shiela St Clair does not fail to entertain us with many bizarre and puzzling happenings.

THE FIRST BOOK OF IRISH BALLADS
Compiled by Daniel O'Keefe and edited with musical arrangements by James N. Healy.

Ballads were made by the people for the people, and they went straight to the hearts of their hearers, who were quick to feel the human emotions—love, hate, pity and fear. This selection chronicles and proclaims a country's sorrows, joys and glories.

THE SECOND BOOK OF IRISH BALLADS

A further selection of ballads with musical arrangements.

IRISH BALLADS AND SONGS OF THE SEA
Compiled by James N. Healy

Our ballads of the sea have a wonderful variety about them, if only for the reason that 'the sea carried our manhood to die in Spain, to fight in France, to be transported to Van Diemen's Land; and following the dreadful days of a famine in the middle of the last century, to become rich in the Golden Land of Americay'. Printed collections of genuine sea ballads are very rare. Musical arrangements are included.

BALLADS FROM THE PUBS OF IRELAND
Compiled by James N. Healy

A thoroughly enjoyable, roistering collection of sad songs, merry lyrics and ballads of love that men roar out with a depth of feeling in the 'pubs' of Ireland.